Marathoning A to Z

500 Ways to Run Better, Faster, and Smarter

Hal Higdon

THE LYONS PRESS

Guilford, Connecticut

An Imprint of the Globe Pequot Press

10 9 8 7 6 5 4 3 2 1

Printed in the United States of America

Photos courtesy of The LaSalle Bank Chicago Marathon

Library of Congress Cataloging-in-Publication Data is available on file.

Contents

Introduction

When we hadn't heard from her in nearly two weeks, Richie wondered, "Where is Anne?" He joked that she might be off somewhere feeding the squirrels. Hydee suggested that Anne (who worked as a fitness instructor for a Detroit YMCA) might be at a health conference learning new exercises to teach us. I kiddingly said that she could be attending a Polish wedding in Hamtramck and hinted that, if we hadn't heard from Anne within a week, we would send out a search party. "I miss her advice," admitted Erika.

When we learned where Anne had been, we all were somewhat chagrined. Within a day of our inquiries, Anne surfaced and informed us that she had undergone emergency surgery. This resulted in a flood of condolence messages directed to the recuperating Anne. "I opened my email box, and 45 greetings popped up," she later told me. We were all Anne's concerned neighbors, but only in cyberspace. Richie lives in Atlanta; Hydee in Vienna, Austria; Erika in Fair Haven, New Jersey. I manage their back-and-forth email messages from my home in Long Beach, Indiana. Among my various writing duties, I host a *Virtual Training* forum on the Internet. We were all members of "Hal Higdon's V-Team" and had V-shirts and singlets to prove it. Sponsored by The LaSalle Bank Chicago Marathon, *Virtual Training* has an unpaid membership of perhaps 10,000 runners, some of them training for that marathon, some for others. On a given day, I might field 20 or 30 messages: questions concerning training or injuries or where to find a good Italian restaurant the night before the race.

I now enjoy dispensing advice on the Internet as much as writing articles for *Runner's World*, or books such as *Marathon: The Ultimate Training Guide*. Yet there's a certain impermanence to cyberwriting. Because of the sheer volume of V-Team messages, comments by me and others move rapidly down and off the computer screen to unseen archival regions. Yes, you can do a "search" and read what I've written about various injuries or how fast and far to do your long runs, but in one recent six-month period, I posted 2,115 comments or answers! That was out of a total of 18,795 postings on *Virtual Training*. Obviously, we are a garrulous bunch.

Marathoning from A to Z is an attempt to gather more than 500 of these postings (the most important and interesting ones) and put them between the covers of a book for easy access, as well as for a more permanent record. Here is a paper trail of my thoughts about running, particularly about running the marathon.

Certainly, the marathon has attained a peak of popularity in 2002 that nobody could have anticipated when I first started running the event four decades earlier. In 1959, when I ran my first marathon, in Boston, only 151 started the race. There were only two or three other marathons in the United States that year and not too many more elsewhere in the world. None of those who ran Boston in 1959 was female, because at the time women actually were prohibited from running races more than a few miles long. By 1980, however, running had experienced a boom, with nearly 8,000 running Boston and dozens, maybe hundreds, of marathons elsewhere. At the 1996 Boston Marathon, 36,000 participated. By the new millennium, fields larger than 25,000 had become routine at marathons in Chicago, New York, Honolulu,

London and Berlin. And many more of those running 26 miles were women. In 1980 the typical marathon had only 10 percent women compared with 38 percent today.

The success of *Virtual Training* partly reflects the success of long-distance running as an important participant sport. But it also reflects the success of technology in bringing us instant information. One attraction of my cyberspace column is that, if you have a training question, you can ask it online and get a quick response. Either I or one of the other been-there-done-that V-Teamers will provide the answer you need. If you're worried whether to do your 20-miler this weekend or next, we'll tell you. If you wonder at what pace to run during your mid-week "sorta-long" runs, you can find out. If you're a newcomer and don't understand the meaning of fartlek, tempo runs, interval training and carbo-loading, I've got the definition on the tip of my keyboard.

I serve as coach not only for the 10,000 or more active V-Teamers, but also for that many or more who follow the various training programs on my separate Web site: www.halhigdon.com. I suggested to a reporter before one recent Chicago Marathon that I probably trained half the runners in the field, "everyone except Khalid Khannouchi." I was being facetious, but maybe not.

Not all the tips offered in this book originated with *Virtual Training*. Some come from my writing in earlier books, or from articles in *Runner's World* and other publications. Still other tips are part of the conventional wisdom that exists around the sport of marathoning. When you've been running for half a century and have finished more than a hundred marathons, you do acquire a lot of information that can be— *should be*—passed on to upcoming generations of runners.

Writing *Marathoning from A to Z* was the best way to accomplish this end, because regardless of the speed and convenience of cyberspace, sometimes it's faster and easier to grab a book off the shelf when you have a specific question about running. Also, not everybody has the cybertools to surf seamlessly through the massive amount of material available now on the World Wide Web. Gathered between the covers of this book is a lot of information on marathon running that you would be hard pressed to find in cyberspace without a better search engine than currently exists. Did you say you had a question about Qualifying for Boston? Flip to the Q chapter and go to page 143. Want to know when to get a Massage or how to treat Blisters? You have the answer in your hands.

So here are more than 500 tips for marathoners, new and old. They do reflect the best of my writing. Before setting you free to browse at will through these alphabetized topics, I must acknowledge that this book would not have been possible without the help and support of my V-Team. Both directly and indirectly, they have inspired *Marathoning from A to Z*. The marathon, it has been said, is a journey, not a destination. I hope you benefit from my thoughts on the experience of running 26 miles 385 yards.

A

is for Aerobic

A

You grade "A" in the marathon as long as you finish. How fast you run the race is not as important as many would think.

A.M.

Most runners train in the morning, for several reasons. It is convenient. It wakes you up and gets you going. It helps you begin the day with a positive attitude. You "get it over with"—and don't have to worry about squeezing in a workout later, when other activities may intrude. It is quieter. Fewer people or machines can get in your way or intrude on your thoughts. You get to see sunrises.

Abs

"Ripped abs" have become *the* goal for many who exercise. Members of Generation X covet well-defined abdominal muscles, also known as having a "six-pack." Although strong stomach muscles certainly are desirable if you're a runner, having that ripped-ab look becomes increasingly immaterial as you run those last six miles in the marathon, your only goal making it to the finish line one way or another.

Accelerate

If you're running a middle-distance race on the track, accelerating suddenly mid-race may allow you to break your opponent and win the race. Accelerating in the middle of a marathon rarely makes sense, even for front-runners. Sudden shifts in pace can waste energy and jeopardize your ability to finish well. A moderate but steady pace will get you to the finish line with the best hope for a good performance.

Acclimatization

Shifting climates or altitudes when you travel can cause discomfort while training and result in slower race times than you had anticipated. When faced with a climate change, adjust your goals accordingly. Usually it is easier to run an unseasonably warm marathon in the fall than in the spring, because you will retain some of the heat resistance garnered while training through a hot summer.

Accumulation

It is the accumulation of training miles over a long period of time that will permit you to get better. Miles run in practice are like dollars saved in the bank.

Achilles

The Greek warrior-hero from Homer's *Iliad*, Achilles was vulnerable only in the heel. An arrow shot by Paris hit Achilles there and killed him. Runners also are vulnerable in their Achilles tendons, which connect heel to calf. Strain your Achilles tendon, and running will become very painful. Speedwork and hill training can cause Achilles tendon injuries; proper stretching and intelligent training can prevent them.

Adapting

Runners who suddenly increase mileage—or plug in more speedwork—often report that they have "heavy legs." They become more easily fatigued. And they may become injured. That is because it takes muscles time to adapt to increased training loads. For that reason, be *very* cautious when changing your training habits. Make only small changes. Some experts suggest increasing mileage by no more than 10 percent a week, but even that may be too much for most runners.

Addiction

Drugs, alcohol, cigarettes—all are considered *negative* addictions because, though they bring temporary pleasure, they also tear down your body and eventually can cause pain and premature death. Running also is an addiction, but a *positive* one. You build your body and improve your health. Running also can help you eliminate the negative addictions from your life.

Advertising

Put your name on your shirt when you run marathons. The spectators will notice and cheer for you by name. Their encouragement can be a big pickup in the closing miles.

Aerobic

Keep your long runs aerobic. Try not to push too hard in workouts or to get out of breath, particularly in the early miles. You'll be able to finish stronger if you start slow. That is true in the marathon itself as much as it is in training.

Agony

The TV sports show *Wide World of Sports* made "the agony of defeat" a catchphrase through its image of a skier tumbling off the end of a ski jump. But the marathon need not be agonizing, as long as you train properly.

Aid Stations

You can drink more if you walk through aid stations during your marathon race, and you won't lose that much time. The slower you are as a runner, the less time you will lose between your running and walking pace.

Aid-Station Strategy

Most runners are right-handed and drift that way when going through aid stations. In races where there are aid stations on both sides of the road, there often is less of a crowd on the left. Also, wait to the end of the aid station to grab your drink, since most runners grab the first cups available. Be alert, so you know whether you're grabbing water or the sports drink.

Alcohol

Having too much to drink, or even hanging around with people who do, is not a good idea. People get killed because they get in a car with a drunk driver. Alcohol can inhibit your performance as a runner because it dehydrates you, not an ideal situation either before a race or a long workout on a hot day. Too much alcohol also can interfere with glycogen storage in your muscles. A moderate amount of alcohol with your meals is not a problem, but stay out of the bars if you want to become a better runner.

Alibis

There should be no alibis offered after you run a marathon. Insufficient training, a pre-race cold or the flu, warm weather, a head wind or an intemperate pace sometimes can conspire to prevent you from running a fast time—or even finishing. But alibis don't count. Nobody wants to hear them. The important thing is that you tried.

Altitude

Flat-country runners who run in the mountains during vacation trips sometimes have problems breathing. Running at altitude is not easy—but it's not that difficult, either, if you approach your High Country training with the correct attitude. So it's a matter of attitude toward altitude. *Simply slow down!* Leave your watch in the hotel. Cut your training pace and walk if you get too much out of breath. Just cover the distance and enjoy the scenery. You can get back into your old training patterns after you head home.

Anabolic Steroids

Athletes in strength sports such as football, baseball or certain field events sometimes take performance-enhancing drugs to improve strength. Elite distance runners also get caught doing the same, resulting in their suspension or banishment from competition. Sadly, the lure of Olympic gold sometimes is irresistible. But for those who have embraced running for its health benefits, it makes absolutely *no* sense to use steroids or other drugs, because of long-range side effects, some of them not yet understood. Consider this: Is taking two minutes off your marathon time worth taking two years off your life?

Anaerobic Threshold

The anaerobic threshold for untrained runners might be 50 percent of maximum; that is, they begin to accumulate lactic acid in their muscles while running at half their maximum heart rate. This forces them to slow down. For an "average" runner, the anaerobic threshold could be 60 to 70 percent, and a "good" runner may still be able to function aerobically at 85 percent of maximum. Top runners push into the world beyond during competition. This permits them to run seemingly endless miles below a five-minute pace without apparent distress. Even less-gifted runners can push their anaerobic threshold to the right of the scale: from 50 percent toward 85 percent. All it takes is intelligent training.

Anti-depressant

Running is the best anti-depressant on the market, with virtually no cost or negative side effects.

Anxiety

Racing can make us nervous. We worry about our ability to finish, or to finish in a time fast enough to repay us for our training. Even in training, we can become anxious when it comes time to run certain distances or workouts. For novice runners, that first 20-miler that comes near the peak of their marathon training may seem like an insurmountable task. But once that task is completed, anxiety vanishes to be replaced by confidence.

Attitude

With the right attitude, anyone can succeed in the marathon and make running fun.

Average

There is no such thing as an average runner. We are all above average.

Awards

Some win cash prizes. Some win medals and trophies. Some win age-group awards, including merchandise. For most of the rest of us, our award is simply having done it.

B

is for Basics

Back-to-Back

Running back-to-back marathons (two marathons within a month of each other) can be a difficult task. The trick is to run one easy and the other hard (or to run both easy). It doesn't matter whether you do the hard one first or second as long as you adjust your training between. Take it *very* easy the week after the first marathon. Do next to nothing the week before the second. If you have time between, do some running, but nothing difficult. Trying to run hard between or in both marathons can set you up for disappointment—and an injury.

Bad Days

Nobody said training for a marathon was easy. Heat and humidity, or a tough course, or too little sleep the night before, or some combination of factors, can convert what should be an easy workout into a struggle. When circumstances conspire against you, relax and throw your training plan out the window—at least for that day. For every bad day running, there is an infinite number of better days.

Bad Marathons

There is no such thing as a bad marathon, only less successful good marathons.

Bad Patch

Frequently in races, runners begin to struggle. They lose rhythm. They experience fatigue not felt before. Their pace slows. Then, suddenly, they recover. The British have an expression for this. They call it going through a "bad patch." Bad patches may be as much psychological as physical. Everybody has them, even the elites. To be a Complete Runner, you need to learn to persevere through bad patches.

Bad Weather

Race-day weather is something we can't control. A bad day (too hot or too cold) can wipe out a whole year of training to set a Personal Record. When you encounter bad weather, you have two options: (1) Skip the race and schedule another on a day when the weather may be better, or (2) lower your time goals and simply enjoy the race as an experience without worrying about how fast you run.

Bandits

Runners who participate in races without properly entering or who use someone else's number are properly branded as "bandits." They cheat every other runner who paid to enter, stealing water at aid stations and support along the course. Switching numbers without permission compromises the results and may cause you and the person whose number you borrowed to be disqualified from future races. Do not cheat your fellow runners by becoming a bandit!

Barefoot

For better foot health, try barefoot running. One problem with today's running shoes is that they encapsulate the foot, preventing any stretching or strengthening of the foot muscles. Pick soft surfaces such as a golf course fairway or a smoothly packed beach, and limit yourself to short distances until your feet get used to running barefoot.

Bargains

Beware of running shoes sold at bargain prices. They may be on the "sale" table because they've been in the store six or more months, during which time they have begun to lose their bounce. The materials used in shoes do deteriorate with age. Be sure you know what you're buying. For this reason, it's also not a good idea to stock up on several pairs of your favorite model before it goes out of style.

Base

Before beginning a new training program, make sure you have an adequate base. Base usually results from having spent several weeks or months when you run relatively long but easy workouts before beginning speed training. This aerobic base allows you to run short distances fast without undue stress. But a base can also consist of speed training before a marathon buildup. The most successful training programs combine speed, distance and rest, but not always at the same times of the year.

Basics

The training basics for the marathon are long runs and rest. You need long runs to improve your endurance. You need rest to do your long runs comfortably. You won't succeed without both basic elements.

Beer

Drinking beer or other alcoholic beverages too soon after a distance race is not a great idea. If you are dehydrated (common after even cool-weather races), the alcohol will dehydrate you further. For that reason, seek water and other fluids immediately after crossing the finish line before heading to the beer tent. Even better, delay any alcohol consumption until dinner much later that night.

Big Marathons

Big marathons are not necessarily better than small marathons. Each has its own appeal. But one advantage for first-time runners of big marathons is more support on the course, more spectators on the course and more runners on all sides of you. If you're planning on finishing in five or six hours, you'll have a lot more company in a big marathon than in a small one.

Black Toes

Black toes occur when blood blisters form under one or more toenails, usually after a long run in ill-fitting shoes. Since feet will swell during long runs, this compounds the problem, particularly in marathon races. Draining the blisters can best be done by a podiatrist, although you may still lose the toenail. To avoid this in the future, be sure to select shoes that fit your feet.

Blending

Tempo runs in the woods, interval workouts on the track, long runs and pace workouts on the road—all are important when it comes to achieving peak performance. Add to that easy runs and total rest. Good training (particularly for more experienced runners) requires a blend of all the elements.

Blisters (causes)

If you want to discover the cause of blisters, first look inside your shoes. Pressure points may be the problem.

Blisters (frequent)

If you're plagued by *frequent* blisters, and the ordinary home remedies don't work, it's time to visit a podiatrist. Bring your running shoes, your socks, anything that might contribute to your problem. Also bring your training log, since a recent increase in distance or a change in training surface may be to blame. Once the podiatrist helps you discover the cause of your blisters, you will be halfway to a solution.

Blood

One way elite athletes improve performance is by removing a quart of blood several months before a major race and getting a transfusion with this same blood later. This is called "blood-doping," and it's considered unethical. The theory is that by adding blood you also add oxygen-carrying red corpuscles. Conversely, if you remove blood, you have fewer of those red corpuscles. This can have a negative (though temporary) effect on your training. Please *do* donate blood occasionally as a humanitarian, but not the last month before an important race.

Brain Training

Not every day is a perfect day for running—or for running as hard a workout as your training plan suggests. When temperatures rise, you may need to cut back both on pace and distance and drink more than normal. If lightning is striking or there's a foot of fresh snow on the ground, maybe today is the day for some alternate training in the gym. Your coach may have prescribed a specific workout, but coaches can't anticipate every problem you might encounter before or during a workout. When in doubt, engage your brain.

Breaking In

Several weeks before your marathon, make sure that you have broken in all the equipment you plan to use in the race: shoes, socks, shorts, singlet. Test them in at least one long run to make sure that they won't cause a blister or chafing that will cause discomfort on race day. Buying new equipment at the marathon Expo is not a good idea—unless you plan to wait to use it after you get home.

Breakfast (daily)

The secret to good nutrition, any dietitian will tell you, is breakfast. So-called "continental breakfasts" featuring coffee and rolls don't provide much in the way of vitamins and minerals. Instead, start the day with a healthy breakfast, which will allow you to maintain energy and avoid hunger pangs. Try a whole-bran cereal with skim milk, and top it off with raisins and bananas and other fruits in season. And don't forget the orange juice. This is a form of carbo-loading that too many runners overlook in their eagerness to get out of the house and off to work.

Breakfast (races)

Deciding what to eat the morning of a race is an individual matter. Habit dictates choices. Some runners feel uncomfortable without something in their stomachs. Others prefer to avoid morning meals. Eating choices depend on how far you plan to race. In races shorter than the half-marathon, food is less a factor. You should have ample energy reserves from your meal the night before. For marathons, you probably do need more carbohydrates, which is one reason pasta parties are popular the night before. Plan to rise at least three hours before the race for a light breakfast that could include coffee or fruit juice and toast or a bagel.

Breaks

It's a good idea to walk before being forced to do so, both in long workouts and in races—particularly marathons. Plan your walking breaks. One strategy would be to run 1 mile; then walk 200 meters (1/8 mile) before starting to run again. Or run 10 minutes and walk 1 minute. Doing it this way is much easier (and more beneficial) than running 20 miles and walking the last 6 in a marathon.

C

is for Challenge

Calorie Burn

Running is the most practical and efficient way for most people to both burn calories and get in shape. With the possible exception of cross-country skiing (for which you need snow), you will burn more calories per hour while running than in any other sport. Running consumes approximately 100 calories for every mile you cover. Run six miles at 10:00 pace, and you can burn 600 calories during an hour's workout. Run faster and you'll burn even more in the same time. Few other sports come even close to that calorie burn.

Calories

An individual who weighs 150 pounds burns approximately 100 calories for every mile run—or walked. How fast you run or walk that mile doesn't matter. You're pushing a certain number of pounds over a certain length of ground. The calorie burn is roughly the same. Of course, if you run faster, you burn more calories in an hour, because you will run *farther* in that hour. Combining diet with exercise is the best way to both limit and burn calories. This is almost the only effective way to permanently lose weight.

Cannot

The word "cannot" should be removed from the vocabulary of all marathoners.

Carbohydrates

Runners need to focus their attention on carbohydrates while training for a marathon—or training for life. Ignore false prophets who claim carbs are bad for you. They're not—as long as you get most of your carbs from breads, fruits and vegetables. The ritualistic pasta party the night before marathons is not without purpose. The ideal diet has 55 percent carbohydrates, 30 percent fats and 15 percent proteins. Stray far from these percentages at your own risk. Avoid fad diets that don't provide enough fuel-efficient carbohydrates to meet your energy needs as a runner.

Carbohydrates (complex vs. simple)

Not all carbohydrates are created equal. Simple carbohydrates include sugar, honey, jam and any food such as sweets and soft drinks that get most of their calories from sugar. Nutritionists recommend that simple carbohydrates form only 10 percent of your diet. Complex carbohydrates—

the starch in plant foods—are what you should concentrate on most if you want to become a successful runner. This includes fruits, vegetables, breads, pasta and legumes.

Challenge

Nobody said running was supposed to be easy. Running is a challenge that we gratefully accept the minute we decide to become marathoners. Sore legs and fatigue often come with the territory. Gradually, over a period of time, running longer and longer distances will become easier for you. Except then you'll want to run *faster,* and it will be back to square one! The fact that running *is* a challenge is part of its appeal. Accept the bad with the good. There's more of the latter.

Charity

If you're looking for motivation, consider running a marathon for charity. More and more individuals now do so. Some simply select a favorite charity and raise money on their own. Others join well-organized programs that provide not only coaching and group workouts, but also fund-raising advice. The Leukemia & Lymphoma Society with its Team in Training

(TNT) is the most visible and successful. In the year 2000, 35,000 TNT runners raised $82.4 million for the organization.

Childbirth (1)

Having a baby is like running a marathon: a combination of joy and pain. It takes time to recover from either experience.

Childbirth (2)

When women return to running after pregnancy, they need to be cautious about not doing too much too soon. They may have gained weight. If they chose not to run during the final months of pregnancy, they may have lost some fitness. And their hormones may be out of balance. New mothers should return to running eagerly, but cautiously, letting their bodies tell them how much they can do.

Choices

At some point we all learn we need to make choices, which sometimes means sacrificing one goal for another. If you're training for a marathon, doing a triathlon or participating in any other sport can compromise your training. And the opposite is also true. Decide what is most important to you at any particular time and focus on that activity if you want to achieve success.

Classes

When signing up for yoga or other classes involving stretching, do *not*, if you're a guy, try to compete with the spaghetti-loose gals in the same class with you. If you try to match their positions and flexibility, you will push yourself into an injury, which is not what you want. For the same reason, gals should not try to compete with hunks lifting weights. We compete against ourselves, not against others.

The Club

If running were easy, everyone would be doing it. Marathoners belong to a very exclusive club.

Clubs

Runners traveling out of town sometimes have trouble finding the best running areas and/or running companions. The best locator is the Road Runners Club of America's Web site: www.rrca.org. The RRCA lists nearly 700 clubs, usually with email addresses of club leaders. I was in Santa Fe, New Mexico, one weekend and located a local runner this way. She took me for a two-hour run on a Friday morning. Another good source is the archive of travel articles by Doug Rennie on www.runnersworld.com.

Clydesdales

Heavy runners—often referred to as "Clydesdales"—have to train more carefully than those who weigh less. A 220-pound runner, regardless of fitness, impacts the pavement much harder than someone weighing 160 pounds. While an 18-week training program might be sufficient for a lightweight athlete training for a marathon, a Clydesdale might want to stretch that program to 24 or even 32 weeks by using more rest days and building mileage much more gradually. Shoe choice also is critical in staying healthy if you're in the upper weight levels.

Cockiness

New York coach Bob Glover claims he did his first marathon on a bet and hit the wall because of youthful cockiness. He now tells runners to take the marathon seriously and train to beat it; otherwise, it will beat you.

Comfort

To select your everyday training pace, be aware of how comfortable you feel while running at different speeds and over different distances. There is a subtle difference between running that is comfortable and running that becomes uncomfortable. Find the zone between, and you can maximize your training. Push too far beyond too often, and you risk injury and the diminished performance level that comes with overtraining.

Comfort Level

While training for a running race, it's important to choose your comfort levels, not merely how many miles to run in training, but how much time to devote to that training. You may be comfortable with a certain level of commitment, but others around you may not. Communication with loved ones while setting training and racing goals is always important.

Competition

While running a marathon, don't worry about other runners around you. In trying to complete 26 miles 385 yards, the only competition is yourself.

Complete Runner

To become a Complete Runner (in caps), you need to test your fitness in a variety of fields. Learn how to train on the track and in the woods as well as on the roads. Compete in shorter-distance races as well as the marathon. Only then will you be able to maximize your ability.

Comprehension

Even after finishing their first marathon, many runners still have trouble comprehending how it is possible to run that far. It really is a long way. But if you keep the faith, you can get there.

Common Sense

The best coach you can have is your own common sense. Both in training and in racing, ask yourself often, "Does this make sense?" Learn from your experiences. One way to improve your common sense is to keep a training diary and refer to it often.

Compromise

It's not wise to run too many races during your marathon buildup, since you risk compromising your long workouts, which are the keys to marathon success.

Concentration

One skill that separates the good runners from the almost-good runners is an ability to concentrate their attention for a full 26 miles 385 yards. You can run faster when you focus your attention on your form and on running as smoothly as possible. It's not easy and requires many miles in practice. One of the best ways to fine-tune concentration skills is to do speedwork on a track.

Conditions

Conditions can make an *enormous* difference on how easy any one workout goes. Whether it's hot or cold or windy or humid can affect not only your times, but also your comfort level. Before chastising yourself for having a bad run, consider the conditions during which you did that run.

Consistency (1)

Consistency and an ability to continue to train uninjured are the most important factors leading to success in running. Build gradually and you will succeed.

Consistency (2)

To perform at a high level, you have to train consistently. There's no substitute for steady training over a long period. Continue to train intelligently at a moderate stress level, and you'll do much better than if you try fancy workouts that may contribute more to your failures than to your success.

Cortisone

Physicians sometimes inject cortisone around an inflamed tendon to reduce swelling. This steroid-based drug is a very effective anti-inflammatory and can provide temporary relief, but, before submitting to the needle, ask the doctor whether you really need it. Cortisone can provide some miracle cures, but overuse can break down tissue and eventually damage the tendon. Accept a cortisone injection only as a last recourse. Seek the cause of the inflammation if you want a lasting cure.

Crash and Burn

Run too fast in the early miles of a marathon and you increase your chances of crashing and burning. The last half-dozen miles will prove *agonizing* if you're reduced to a near walk.

But the same is true in training. Build gradually from a solid training base before doing too many hard workouts that can cause a similar crash (injury) or burn (fatigue).

Creatine

Despite the hype about certain baseball players using creatine (creatine monohydrate), research suggests little benefit for runners who take this expensive supplement designed to improve strength. The disadvantage is that you may gain 10 pounds (much of it fluid) that you will have to carry through the marathon. There is also the risk of cramps. And nobody yet knows what side effects, particularly to the liver and kidneys, you may encounter 20 or 30 years down the road from this or any other "performance-enhancing" supplement.

Cross-Country

Fear of the unknown and fear of injury often prevent marathoners from running cross-country, either racing or training on trails. Granted, for those who train only on smooth and flat pavement, uneven and hilly courses *do* pose some risk. Yet cross-country offers many scenic options for those not afraid to muddy their shoes. The least-trod trail often is the prettiest trail, providing scenic venues that less adventuresome athletes never see. Perhaps more important, moving your training from hard pavement to soft trails can help you avoid injuries and increase your speed, so that when you do run road races, you can improve your performances.

Cross-Training

If you are training for a marathon, the purpose of cross-training is not to build muscles. (You may build the wrong muscles.) Its purpose is to offer a relaxing workout between hard runs to both build and maintain your aerobic capacity. Easy swimming, cycling or even walking is sufficient for most cross-training days. Cross-train too much and you may be too fatigued to train properly on the days you do run.

Crowd Support

Never underestimate the power of the crowd. People cheering can inspire you to efforts you never dreamed of. But don't become too inspired by the cheers of the crowd, particularly in the early miles. You don't want the enthusiasm rained on you by spectators to push you faster than your carefully planned pace. The crowds will get you through the first 20 miles, but from that point on, you need to dig down deep and earn victory for yourself.

Crying

It is okay to cry while running—particularly in the finishing chute (if your body has any fluids left).

Cumulative Fatigue

While running gurus promote the importance of "negative splits" (wherein you run the second half of your race faster than the first), that's not always easy to accomplish. It's natural that you might slow your pace as the race gets longer. It's the result of cumulative fatigue. No surprise there. But it's also tougher to recover from races and long runs in which cumulative fatigue takes over. As mileage builds in your training program, you may find it necessary to schedule more rest days to allow your body more recovery time.

D
is for Distance

Darters

The most despised runners in road racing are the darters. These are runners who dodge and dart in crowded fields, trying to make up ground after positioning themselves too far back at the start. In getting around other runners, they move diagonally back and forth, cutting others off and forcing them to slow down. It's dangerous, because you may trip yourself or others. If caught behind, relax; the crowd eventually will thin, allowing you to run at your own pace. Or move to the far left or right, since passing is often easier on the edges of crowded fields.

Defining Success

Anyone can set a Personal Record just by showing up at a starting line. It may be a P.R. for your career, your present age group, or the month of January. You set the rules by which you define success.

Diagnosis

One means of diagnosis of any injury is to ask yourself the question: Does it feel worse or better at the end of the run? If it's worse, you may need to take time off from running.

Dietitians

Learn to eat properly, not merely before marathons, but all the time. A lot of runners use personal trainers and massage therapists and podiatrists and overlook the fact that a registered dietitian sometimes can be the most important sports professional in improving both their health and their performances.

Difficulty

The most difficult mile is not the 26th mile of the marathon, but the first mile you run in training that hints that you might be able to finish a marathon.

Distance

World-record holder Khalid Khannouchi claims that it is not the competition that you should fear, but the distance. "I fell in love with the distance," says Khannouchi, "and the marathon became my favorite event."

Double Workouts

Running twice a day is probably counterproductive for most runners. Unless you're training for the Olympics, double

Drink Right

You need to learn how to drink properly, and that's why you should practice drinking during your long workouts. Here are some drinking tips for the long run:

1. **Drink before running.** Drink adequately and drink often up until two hours before you run. Excess body water will be passed as urine. Two hours before, however, stop drinking to allow your system to clear.

2. **Drink while you run.** Just before beginning to run, start drinking again. Once you're moving, you'll sweat off any excess liquid before it reaches your kidneys. This is very important during warm weather. You'll run faster and recover sooner. Carry a water bottle if necessary.

3. **Walk to drink.** Don't try to gulp fluids down while running. You'll be able to drink more if you stop or at least walk. You'll lose less time than you think. My son Kevin once ran a 2:18 marathon and qualified for the Olympic Trials by walking through every aid station on a warm day.

4. **Drink after running.** Drink as soon as you stop, but even after your initial thirst is quenched, you still need to keep drinking. One sign of adequate hydration is clear urine.

workouts are simply not worth the time and effort. Not only do you increase your risk of injury, but running becomes a chore rather than a pleasure.

Doubters

When asked by doubting others why you are running a marathon, tell them, "Because I can!"

Downhill

Running downhill can be more difficult than running uphill, particularly if the descent is steep. You want to take advantage of the down side of a hill to regain time lost on the up side, but running too hard can be jarring to the muscles. Braking, meanwhile, has its own set of problems. Relax and let the hill carry you down, then try to regain your regular pace as soon as possible after you hit the flat. Experience gathered by running hills in training will help you cope with the downs as well as the ups.

Drafting

Cyclists appreciate the advantage of drafting. By letting the lead cyclist break the wind, others can match his speed with significantly less energy output. It works with runners too, if you're running into a head wind, but more important than any physical benefit is the *psychological* benefit of letting someone else set the pace. With your mind free, you can relax until the closing sprint. It's somewhat impolite to draft another runner without permission, however.

Dreams

Keep your dream in front of you. Never let go of it regardless of how far-fetched it might seem.

Drinking

Runners understand the importance of drinking in a marathon, particularly on a warm day. But you also need to drink while training. Not only will drinking fluids make your workouts more comfortable, it also will teach you *how* to drink and *how often* to drink. Drinking on the run is a science—and so you need to practice, particularly during long training runs.

E

is for Exercise

The LaSalle Bank Chicago Marathon

Easy

Running a marathon can never be easy. If it were easy, the challenge would be gone. But by learning to train properly, you can increase your enjoyment and make completing 26 miles 385 yards easier than you ever thought possible

Economy

Exercise scientists like the term "economy" when they describe fast runners. You've seen economical runners; they skim over the ground and seem to waste little energy as they fly past you at a speed you can barely imagine. Some of the economy possessed by fast runners is natural; some of it is developed during training. If you can improve your economy of motion (no easy task), you can be a faster runner too.

Elementary

"Elementary, my dear Watson," Sherlock Holmes used to tell his partner in solving crimes, and becoming a better runner is elementary too. You gradually add miles to your training. You run some of those miles faster. You program rest into your schedule at appropriate times. You wear proper equipment. And if you do suffer an injury, you learn from your training mistakes. Soon, running becomes much easier—and more fun too.

Elimination

If you are interested in marathon success, you may need to eliminate some of the other activities—such as strength training or cross-training—from your regular routine. It's not that much of a problem in the early stages of your training, but as the long runs build to beyond 13 miles, stress also increases. That's when you begin to run out of both time and energy for non-running activities. Putting a temporary hold on them may be necessary to run your best marathon times.

Endurance

It takes a high degree of endurance to succeed in the marathon. Fortunately, endurance is a skill that responds to intelligent training. The best way to increase endurance is to increase volume. Within certain limits, the more miles you can run, the more you can improve your endurance.

Exercise Etiquette

Not all people who exercise display courtesy to their fellow exercisers. Here are some sins committed by those of us who sweat:

- **Walkers:** Hogging the roadway or pathway is bad manners. Moving slowly is not the issue; walking two-, three- or four-abreast is. Sudden shifts in direction can prove a problem for trailing runners.

- **Cyclists:** Pack cycling is as bad as pack running, but the main etiquette sin of people on bikes is the belief that they are immune to traffic laws. On tight paths, skimming past runners and walkers without warning is both foolish and dangerous.

- **Inline skaters:** Skaters often can't make up their minds whether to obey the rules of foot-exercisers or wheeled-exercisers—or they don't know either rules. Rookie skaters often take up too much room on the road with their side-to-side movements.

- **Runners:** Like walkers and cyclists, they often cluster in groups and irritate drivers, causing road rage that later may be directed at others. Bothered by the behavior of the three groups above, runners sometimes feel they invented fitness, and everyone else go home!

- **Indoor exercisers:** A different set of rules takes priority once you enter the gym. Failing to towel off your sweat after departing an exercise machine is one sin. Hogging that machine is another. Failing to regularly change T-shirts offends those forced to exercise in your pungent wake.

Eventually, most walkers, cyclists, skaters, runners and indoor exercisers discover that there is an Exercise Etiquette that will allow them to do their own thing while allowing others to do their things as well.

Energy

Training too hard can drain energy. Even though you get through your daily workouts and complete the miles prescribed in your training program, you may feel fatigued both before and after workouts. You may also need more sleep, yet at the same time you will have trouble getting to sleep. To conserve energy, choose a sensible training program, eat a diet with plenty of carbohydrates, and get to bed early each night.

Enjoyment

Often the enjoyment in running a marathon is the training before and the memory after.

Entry Blank

Even though you sent your money in months before, bring your entry blank with you to the race. Often there's some important bit of information related to times or places that you will need to know. Keep all other information related to the race in a single place or file folder where you can easily find it when needed. This includes the confirmation card that you need to turn in to receive your number without inconvenience.

Equipment

Billy Joel sang it in one of his songs: "Don't waste your money on a new pair of speakers; you get more mileage from a cheap pair of sneakers." Running shoes are *not* inexpensive, costing near $100, but equipment for running certainly costs less than that for almost any other sport. Nevertheless, don't go too cheap. Spend enough for clothing and equipment so you can run in comfort.

Estimates

You need to make a realistic estimate of how fast you expect to run in the marathon. One formula is to multiply your 10-K time by 4.66, although a more conservative approach for novice runners is to multiply that 10-K times 5. There are also numerous prediction charts available both in books and on-line. Once you have an idea of the pace you plan to run in the marathon, you can train at that pace at appropriate times.

Even Pace

Starting fast and finishing slow is not much fun in a marathon. Even pace usually wastes less energy and results in a faster time. Just by maintaining a smooth and steady pace, you'll find yourself passing a lot of impetuous people in the closing miles.

Exam

The marathon is one exam on which you can't cheat. If you fail to do the proper mileage, you'll receive a low grade. Cramming doesn't work, either. Force too many miles into the last month before the big test, and you'll probably run slower rather than faster. The best approach is to begin your training well before the race, which will allow you to spread your "study" time over a longer period. A high grade on the test will be the result.

Excessive Pain

Anytime you increase your training level, pain may develop. It goes with the territory. However, if the pain is excessive, you probably need to be evaluated by a sports-medicine specialist. Perhaps there's some muscle or foot imbalance that is at the root of your pain. Cure it, and you can run free again.

Excuse

Training for the marathon offers us the excuse to get together on weekends with like-minded runners with the same goals. After the marathon is over, a lot of runners miss this opportunity for social contact, even if it's only once a week. For those who have done previous marathons, it is often the training for them that is more fun than actually racing 26 miles.

Excuses

"I don't have time to run." "I don't like to sweat." "Running will destroy my knees." "I might have a heart attack." It's easy to invent excuses *not* to exercise. You hear them all the time from well-meaning friends, who may be jealous of your fitness but don't want to admit it. Ignore people who try to coax you back onto the sidelines.

Exercise

One of the best ways to both maintain and improve your health is with regular bouts of exercise. Exercising aerobically three to five days a week for 20 to 60 minutes will improve your basic fitness, extend your life by several years and also make you feel and look better. Add two days of strength training to complete the picture. Running is one of the most efficient forms of exercise for physical fitness.

Exercise Machines

One distinct advantage of exercise machines is that you can focus on a specific muscle group and avoid stressing others. This is important when recovering from injuries. However, be cautious about which machines you select for your strength-training routine. You don't want to develop antagonistic muscles that can interfere with your running stride. When in doubt, see a strength coach who understands the sport of running. This is essential. Not all strength coaches do.

Experiment

Not every training program is suited for every runner. Sometimes you have to experiment and play around to find out what works best for you.

Extra Training

More isn't always better when it comes to improving your marathon time. While increasing your weekly miles will work at first, you eventually reach a point at which you not only get no better, but your performances begin to deteriorate because of excessive fatigue. Finding exactly the right mileage that will allow you to maximize your training time is one of the most difficult tasks for any runner to achieve.

F
is for
Finishing

Fad Diets

Good nutrition will get you to the starting line and help provide energy to reach the finish line. Fad diets will not. Some examples of fad diets include the Dr. Atkins Diet, the Zone Diet, and other variations of the 40/30/30 theme. Because of their focus on protein vs. carbohydrates, they do not provide enough energy for endurance athletes.

Failure

I've crashed during races on several occasions, particularly early in my career. I failed to finish my first three marathons and barely got to the finish in the fourth. My problem was that I was trying to *win* the races, not finish. In one marathon in California, I was leading at 20 miles and sitting on the curb at 22. Bad things sometimes happen to good people. I know much more about training now than I did then, one reason that I have had more recent success. Learn from your failures, and eventually you can eliminate them.

Fartlek

This form of training, popular with cross-country athletes, gets its name from the Swedish word for "speed-play"—and that's how to do fartlek. Play around by surging at different speeds over different distances, slowing to recover between. Fartlek is best done in the woods or on cross-country trails where you are unaware of the exact distances being run. Even if you are not on a cross-country team, you can benefit by doing this form of training that can either be the easiest or the hardest workout of the week, depending on how you do it.

Fashion

One woman runner I know, who loves chic running clothes, has the right attitude. "If I can't be fast, at least I can be fashionable," she says.

Fast-Twitch Muscles

Not all of us are born physiologically equal. Some possess more speed than others. Invariably, their muscles have more fast-twitch than slow-twitch muscles. Everybody is blessed with both, but some have more of one than the other. This is why some succeed as sprinters and others succeed as distance runners. Fast-twitch muscles fire quickly but also quickly exhaust their glycogen. They are good for short bursts of energy. Slow-twitch muscles contract more slowly, but they maintain that contraction for a longer period of time. Training helps fast-twitch athletes go farther and slow-twitch athletes run faster.

Finding Hills

Runners who live in flat areas of the country often have trouble finding hills to follow the prescriptions of coaches, such as Arthur Lydiard, who consider hill training essential to success. Inventiveness is the key. Run on bridges and overpasses. Use the ramps of parking garages. Use stairwells in tall buildings. Olympian Marty Liquori used to run up the stadium steps at the University of Florida. "If Lydiard lived in Gainesville," claimed Liquori, "he'd have his athletes run stadium steps."

Fine-Tuning

One way to fine-tune your training is with speedwork, whether repeats, intervals, fartlek or tempo runs. You need to teach your legs what it feels like to run fast. You can improve your times by slowly increasing distance, but eventually improvement ceases and you will hit a plateau. Speedwork can help move you off that plateau—as long as you insert it into your training routine cautiously.

Finisher Medal

The medal hung around your neck after you cross the finish line of your first marathon is, indeed, a very special award. Compare it to the degree you got for graduating from college. Wear it proudly—for about 24 hours. (That includes to work the next day.) Then put your medal away, or hang it on the wall with your finishing photo. You earned this one!

Finishing

If you are a first-timer, finishing the marathon should be your *only* goal. Don't set yourself an artificial time goal that can only add stress to your race, both while preparing for it and afterward. Save time goals for later marathons. Regardless of a first-time runner's fitness, wisdom dictates running at least a half hour slower than his or her capability. That way, the first-timer is guaranteed two things: (1) a comfortable finish and (2) a Personal Record for the next marathon because the first one was so slow.

Fit (shoes)

The farther you run—either training or racing—the more important it is that your shoes fit correctly. Make absolutely sure that the shoes feel comfortable when you try them on in the shoe store. Allow extra room in the toe box, but too-large shoes will offer as many problems as too-small shoes. Have your feet measured, even if you think you know your shoe size. (You may have larger feet than you think.) Athletic shoes are notorious for being small, so don't be concerned if the running-store salesman suggests you buy running shoes a half size or more larger than your normal street-shoe size.

Fitness

Whether or not your immediate goal is a fast 5-K time or completing a marathon, your subliminal goal should be improved physical fitness. The miles run and pounds lifted while young will pay dividends decades later when your overall fitness allows you to enjoy a longer and a healthier life.

Flat Feet

Having very flat feet can be a problem if you are a runner, but so can high arches. We live with what we are born with. Paavo Nurmi, the "Flying Finn," was flat-footed yet won more Olympic medals than any other athlete. Proper shoe selection and, in extreme cases, orthotics can cure most foot problems caused by footplant.

Focus

If you want to excel at the marathon, you have to focus exclusively on that event. Keep your eyes on your most important goal.

Fools

The marathon is not a race that tolerates fools easily. You have to prepare, and you have to prepare properly. If you shortcut your training, you can still enjoy this year's marathon as an Experience, but running your best race may be an elusive goal.

Forward, March

Sometimes we *lose* time while training. A summer cold. A nagging injury. A vacation or business trip that causes us to miss an essential workout. The initial impulse of many runners is to make up lost miles, but missed miles are something you can't always control. Rather than double up on workouts and perhaps trigger another setback, don't worry about what's past. Don't look back; look forward.

Finding Time

Because of the demands of family and business, finding time to train often is the biggest problem in achieving marathon success, or success in any fitness-related activity. Here are some time-grabbing tips that will help you get ready to run 26 miles:

- **Make running a priority.** Plan your day around your exercise. When setting your calendar for the day, week or month, first figure out when you can most likely run; then schedule other activities around it.

- **Talk to people.** While doing this planning, communicate to family, friends and business associates why this is important to you. Let them know why you can't make that 8:00 AM appointment. Communication is particularly important between spouses. Give some to get some.

- **Run in the morning.** That guarantees you get your workout in for the day. If you're suddenly forced to work late, that important mid-week workout won't suddenly go out the window. Lunchtime is also good for quick runs.

- **Become a weekend warrior.** Save your toughest training for the weekends, when you have more time. That's one reason that, in my training programs, I place two of the toughest (and longest) workouts on Saturdays and Sundays.

- **Take days off.** As the marathon approaches and miles build, consider stealing some vacation time. In my program, the mid-week "sorta-long" runs peak at 10 miles, not easy for those with 9-to-5 jobs. If you can't spare a vacation day, how about a half day? Or arrive at work at 10:00 in return for a promise to stay late later.

It's not always easy to find time to train, but nobody claims completing a marathon is supposed to be easy.

Flu

Coming back too soon after the flu is not a wise idea. Sometimes a virus can compromise your immune system for two to four weeks. If you try to resume training at the same level after a period of illness, you may be setting yourself up for another under-the-weather bout. Running through a cold sometimes is okay, but if the "cold" includes a high temperature that results in your taking antibiotics, you need to be *very* cautious about returning too soon.

Food Choices

It's not easy to decide what, and how much of "what," to eat each day, particularly while exercising or trying to lose weight. Getting the right balance of carbohydrates, fats, and protein requires paying attention to what you put in your mouth, particularly if you're counting calories. If you're worried about your diet, consider obtaining professional help. Even if you're already following a healthy diet, a registered dietitian can help with suggestions and advice. It may be the best money you spend as a runner.

Footplant

Different runners have different footplants, dictated by how the parts of their body fit together. Fast runners usually land mid-foot, the point just behind the ball of the foot. They then drop down onto their heel, allowing their body to glide above a foot planted firmly on the ground before they push off with the toes. Some land more forward on the ball; others land more flat-footed on the heel. If you have an imperfect footplant, you may need to see a podiatrist for orthotics. The worst you can do for your footplant is to try to adjust your landing to accommodate what you think other runners do.

The Force

Once you make a commitment to run a marathon, you will discover yourself guided by an inner force that you previously may never have known existed. When things get tough, you can tap into this force. Once the marathon is over, you will know that you can get through whatever else life puts in your path.

Form

If you want to improve your running form, try to imagine yourself running across a glass table.

Fractures

All stress fractures heal differently. Although a knowledgeable physician can offer an educated guess as to how soon you can return to running, it is, at best, just that: a *guess*. Don't risk a relapse by returning too quickly. Before resuming running, try to determine the cause of the stress fracture: Too much mileage? An uneven gait? Insufficient stretching? If you can learn from your injury, you may be able to avoid the next one.

Free Advice

Be careful which experts you listen to. You can get free advice from running friends and in running stores, but following such advice is risky, particularly in the area of injuries. I don't know too many trained medical specialists who work in running stores.

Free Weights

Exercise machines are great for isolating specific muscles, but free weights such as barbells offer you a better total body workout, exercising additional muscles in additional ranges of motion. Proper form is essential, however, if you want to avoid injuring yourself. Instruction from a knowledgeable strength trainer can help you avoid mistakes.

The Fridge

In seeking motivation to stick with your running, don't overlook your friendly family refrigerator. Along with all those magnets holding pictures of your kids, find space to post your training schedule. Mark your miles run each day, if necessary. It will serve as a reminder of what you have done and what you plan to do.

Friendships

Special friendships emerge during the course of 26 miles. These friendships may be fleeting but are no less real. No introductions, no conversations. You run together, pushing each other over many miles. Sometimes you separate, only to come together later on. When you're in the chute—if your new friend is still around—you look over and say, "Great race," and head your separate ways.

G

is for Goals

Gains

Gains differ from goals. Goals are what you *hope* to achieve. Gains are what you *do* achieve!

Game Plan

Each race requires its own game plan. Whether the course is hilly or flat, whether the weather is hot or cold, whether you are running for fun or planning a peak performance—all dictate how you run. Consider your game plan well before going to the starting line. The more important the race, the more thought should be involved.

Gear Check

Several weeks before the marathon, check your gear. Have you replaced the high-mileage shoes you wore all through training? Do so well before race day to ensure a proper fit. Test your race uniform as well while there's still time to consider a replacement.

Gels

The most important invention of the 20th century was not—as some people think—atomic energy, the Internet, or the pill, but, rather, gels, those gelatin packs that runners use for extra energy in marathons. Each pack carries about 100 calories, or enough to provide energy for another kilometer, perhaps another mile. Use safety pins to clip them waist-high to your singlet, tucking them into your shorts. Or buy shorts with wide pockets. Wash the gel down with water for best results.

Genetics

Your ability to achieve success in the marathon—or any other sport—depends greatly on your genetics. Today's marathon champions are slim and short, good for winning 26-mile races, though not for becoming pro football or basketball stars. If you want to be a great runner, carefully choose your parents. What you do with your genetics, however, is up to you.

Gloves

Cheap, cotton gloves can be the runner's best friend during races run on cold days, because you can discard them if the weather warms. But various synthetic-fiber gloves are better since they usually are thin enough to tuck into your shorts after you warm, or to wear beneath an outer pair of gloves on really cold days.

Glycogen

Glycogen is the sugar-like substance (actually a polysaccharide) that serves as the main fuel for our muscles when we exercise. It is stored in the liver and in the muscles. When you run long distances, you begin to deplete your glycogen stores and eventually run out of energy. This is what causes runners to "hit the wall" in a marathon. Proper nutrition coupled with intelligent training allows you to improve your ability to utilize glycogen without crashing.

Goals

If you set flexible goals, you can never be disappointed.

Goals (mid-race)

When the running gets tough toward the end of the marathon, setting short-term goals can keep you going; aid station-to-aid station, mile-to-mile, kilometer-to-kilometer, block-to-block, that light post only a few steps away.

Gratefulness

Be grateful that you are healthy enough to be able to train for a marathon.

Goal Setting

If you have just become a runner, setting goals is one way to motivate yourself to excellence. In doing so, consider the following three strategies:

- **General goal:** What do you expect to achieve by becoming a runner? Weight loss? Fitness? Fun? Camaraderie? Define what it is, and you may have an easier time setting your other goals.

- **Short-range goal:** For many, contemplating the completion of a 26-mile run may be just *too much.* Plus, it's too early to start the 18-week countdown. A good interim goal is a 5-K or 10-K or a similar medium-distance race.

- **Long-range goal:** In many respects, this is the easy one. The marathon is an excellent ultimate goal that motivates many to start moving. You don't have to accomplish a marathon finish this year, or even next, but in pursuing your other goals, keep your eye on this end.

Group Support

One reason to join a training class is to tap into the group support you will get from others of equal ability, or lack of that ability.

67

Group Running

Running with a partner or a group can make running more enjoyable. You can gain additional knowledge about the sport, but you also can occupy your mind and make the miles pass faster. Joining a group, you'll make new friends and maintain motivation. Check your local running store for leads to running clubs in your area, or surf into www.rrca.org for a list of more than 600 clubs and contacts throughout the United States.

Guesswork

By picking a proven training program, you eliminate the guesswork from your marathon preparation.

Guidelines

To become a better runner, you need to: (1) adopt a proper diet, (2) lower body fat, (3) avoid smoking and heavy drinking, (4) obtain adequate sleep and (5) exercise regularly. Do that, and you also can add years to your life.

H

is for Health

Hard/Easy

Most training schedules for experienced runners follow the hard-easy pattern, which features a hard day followed by one or more easy days before running hard again. A hard day could be speedwork or a long run. An easy day could be a few miles jogging or complete rest. That doesn't mean you can't do two or more hard days in a row, but you need a reason to do so.

Head

When it comes to running form, the head serves as keystone for the rest of the body. Allow your head to wander and your body will wander with it, causing you to drift back and forth along the road wasting energy. Focus your gaze approximately 10 meters in front of you, and use your eyes to anchor your head in a relaxed position.

Headsets

Running while wearing a headset can help alleviate boredom, but it can divert your attention too much, which can be dangerous. The Road Runners Club of America recommends not wearing headsets, believing runners need to be aware of their surroundings: "Using headsets, you lose an important sense: your hearing." Stay alert and remain aware of what's going on around you. The more aware you remain, the less vulnerable you are to attack. Exercise good judgment anytime you wear a headset while you run.

Health

Good health is a precious gift, a gift to be honored and certainly never to be taken for granted.

Heart Rate

Well-conditioned athletes tend to have lower heart rates than sedentary individuals, but females often have higher heart rates than males, and younger people higher heart rates than older people. A *very* high heart rate (200 or more) may be a warning sign of heart disease. Obtaining an exercise stress test is one way to accurately determine your maximum heart rate and discover if you have any underlying heart problems that may require treatment.

Heart-Rate Formulas

Various formulas have been proposed for predicting maximum heart rate. One is 220 minus your age. A more accurate formula for fit individuals is 200 minus half your age, but if you're using formulas to predict maximum heart rate, you're guessing. One way to measure maximum heart rate is to enter a 5-K or 10-K race wearing a heart-rate monitor and see what your pulse reaches in the last 200 meters. A safer way would be to take a maximum stress test on a treadmill, administered by a professional.

Heat and Humidity

High temperatures and humid breezes offer a double dose of disaster for runners trying to train through the summer. Even when the temperature is relatively low, moist weather can increase your stress level and threaten your health. When faced with these twin tortures, slow your pace despite what your training program says.

Help

Regardless of age, gender, race, creed or physical ability, every marathon runner has a single goal: to reach the finish. To that end, we help each other in our quest, because that helps all of us reach our mutual goal.

High Country

When traveling to the High Country, run at a slower pace. The thin air will make breathing difficult if you run too hard. Figure the length of time it would take you to do your workout at sea level; then run that length of time without worrying about distance. Take it easy the first two or three days at altitude until you begin to acclimatize. Finding flat ground also may be a problem, so stay relaxed both going up and coming down hills.

High Temperatures

You can sometimes run through a cold and even relieve some of the symptoms, but if you have a high temperature, do *not* run. You may increase your chance of injury while in a weakened condition and compromise your immune system, causing problems that may last not merely weeks, but months.

Hill Substitutes

Flatlanders often are frustrated in their attempts to find quad-strengthening hills for their training. Indoor substitutes would include stair-climbing machines and treadmills on which the incline can be changed. Climbing real stairs—

either a stairwell indoors or a stadium outdoors—is another option along with ramps of parking garages and bridges over expressways. Even flat parts of the country often have hilly areas nearby if you're willing to drive to them.

Hitting the Wall

Exercise scientists inform us that after about two hours of running—20 miles for a top runner—the body runs out of glycogen, the energy source that fuels the muscles. With glycogen depleted, the body begins burning fat, a *much* less efficient fuel source. Running becomes more difficult; thus, runners "hit the wall." With proper training and careful marshaling of your energy resources, you can hurdle this wall and achieve peak performance.

Hunger

New runners sometimes experience hunger pangs after they have been running for several hours, particularly in a marathon. But be careful about what you eat or drink on the run, because it may upset your stomach. Experiment with different refueling strategies. The more you practice eating before and during your runs, the easier it will be to deal with hunger pangs.

Hydration

Our body's air-conditioning system depends on water. Allow yourself to become dehydrated and you can overheat even on a cool day. Proper hydration, therefore, is a necessary technique to master if you want to achieve success in the marathon.

Hypothermia

Low body temperature is called hy*po*thermia. Its opposite, high body temperature, is referred to as hy*per*thermia. Both can be dangerous to your health. Dress properly, drink ample fluids, and pay attention to weather conditions to keep your body temperature at a safe level.

Happiness Is

- a long run through a pleasant area with friends who share the same fitness goals.
- a new pair of shoes at the start and a free T-shirt at the finish.
- the sense of accomplishment that stays with you for hours, days and months.
- hearing people say, "You ran how far?"

- when *Runner's World* declares Pop Tarts a healthy, guilt-free snack.

- seeing your spouse at mile 16 of a 20-mile run. And she has cold Gatorade!

- knowing that by 8:00 on a Sunday morning, you have already had a full workout.

- looking at old photos of you before you became a runner.

- seeing another runner coming toward you at 6:00 in the morning and realizing you're not the only crazy person working out at this ungodly hour.

- realizing that your body can accomplish more than you ever imagined.

- wearing the finisher's medal while walking back to the hotel and fielding congratulations from spectators.

- a step-back week after a hard 20-miler.

- being curled up with a cup of coffee and the newspaper with eight miles behind you—all before the kids wake up.

- having a three-year-old who insists on stretching with you.

- the first time you see your breath on a cool October morning.

- having a body capable of carrying you any distance, be it 26.2 miles or just from the bed to the bathroom.

- a soothing wind at your back and a soft surface beneath your feet.

I

is for Interval Training

I

Marathon running is an "I" sport. There are very few "others" who can provide much more than applause once you step onto the course to run 26 miles 385 yards. Make this your motto: *I* have to train for this sport. *I* have to run the race. *I* deserve all the success I achieve.

Ibuprofen

Many runners use ibuprofen as a pain reliever before long runs or in the marathon itself. This may not be wise. Ibuprofen is an NSAID (non-steroidal anti-inflammatory drug). The fact that it reduces inflammation is the main reason ibuprofen is useful in treating certain injuries. But masking pain is not always a good idea, since it can convert a bad injury into a worse injury. A greater problem (particularly if you take the drug before marathons) is that it can cause gastric distress, sending you into the bushes. Side effects not only include irritation of the lining of your stomach, but ibuprofen taken in excess also can damage your kidneys and liver. These problems occur most often in association with dehydration; thus, the drug is most dangerous on long runs and in fast races. To avoid problems, use ibuprofen *after* you run and in combination with food.

Imagination

In planning your training for the marathon or other races, you're limited only by your imagination in how you package your long runs, your speed workouts and your rest days. However, sometimes it helps to have the support of a good coach.

Impact

Unlike football or other sports in which players collide, running is a low-impact sport. But the impact of the foot hitting the ground occurs over and over and over during the course of running 26 miles 385 yards. That is why shoes to a runner are as important as a helmet to a football player.

Improvement

Gains become more difficult the longer you've been running and the closer you come to your ultimate potential. Age also can be a factor in limiting your ability to improve. Most runners reach their physical maturity and achieve their fastest running times between the ages of 20 and 40. Yet others, who may have started running later in life, can continue to improve on their Personal Records into their 50s and 60s and still keep running at an age when most people have resigned themselves to rocking chairs.

Improving

It's not easy to improve as a runner. You need to work at it. If you're running 20 miles a week and want to get better, you may need to increase your commitment to 30 miles a week, and eventually 40 or more miles a week. You may need to do speed training, which means becoming accustomed to running on tracks or in the woods as well as on roads. And you also may need to train smarter, the ultimate route to success.

Indoors

When the cold winds of winter blow, it's wise to have an indoor option—even if for only a day while a blizzard rages. A treadmill, an exercise cycle, a strength-training routine, a membership in a health club, can get you through those days when no one wants to run outdoors. This includes very hot days as well.

Injuries

If you want to have a long running career, determine what activities most often cause you to become injured; then avoid them.

Innovation

Tricky training programs don't work. Steady miles do.

Inspiration (1)

When training fails, you can always turn to inspiration in the closing miles of a marathon. But training usually works better.

Inspiration (2)

Become an inspiration to others. When I was in my 20s, I met a racewalker in his 40s who impressed me with his physical fitness. He inspired me to be equally fit by the time I reached his age—and I was. Then I looked ahead to runners in their 60s for inspiration to stay in shape. Now that I have passed their age, I find that I can become an inspiration for younger runners seeking the secrets of longevity and good health.

Instant Gratification

There is no instant gratification in marathon running. You can't buy success at your local running store or download it off the Internet. Success in the marathon occurs only after weeks, months and maybe even *years* of hard work. Ironically, this is part of the marathon's great appeal: You get only what you work for.

Intensity

The most common cause of running injuries is intensity. Too much speedwork and high-mileage training can cause the body to break down. Ironically, this same type of training can also allow you to achieve your greatest success. The secret is to insert enough intensity into your training that you improve, but not so much that you injure yourself and undo all the good you've done.

Interest

Putting miles in your training log is like putting money in the bank; you begin to draw interest on it immediately.

Interval Training

A typical interval workout is running 10 × 400 meters, then jogging or walking 200 to 400 meters between. This is very similar to running repeats of a specific distance several times at a fast pace, except the interval *between* the repetition distance is closely controlled. This is where this form of training gets its name. Interval training is a very effective way to improve both speed and performance.

J

is for Jogging

Jay-Running

When crossing a street or highway, either at the corner or in the middle of the block, be very cautious. Look both ways for approaching cars and maybe pause to wait for the light to change from red to green, even though it's going to make your split for that mile somewhat slower. Jay-running can be dangerous. It hurts to get hit by a car.

Jealousy

Although you may have turned your life around by losing weight, starting to run and eliminating old bad habits, not everybody will appreciate your new lifestyle since it may reflect on their current lifestyle. They may make negative comments about your being a runner. Shrug this off as jealousy, but don't argue with them and don't lecture. Your true friends will appreciate what you're doing, and some of them may even be inspired to follow your example. As for the rest, you can still stay in touch by sending them cards every Christmas, even if you no longer hang out with them in the bars Friday nights because you have to get up early to run the next morning.

Jerks

The era when people in passing cars rolled down the windows to scream profanities at runners has generally passed, because there are so many of us. But only generally. There remain jerks everywhere who, upon encountering a runner on the road, feel obliged to vent their anger. Don't incite these jerks to further anger or become more of a target for their rage. Ignore them. Keep on striding. They can be dangerous.

Jet Lag

When traveling afar, contemporary wisdom suggests that you need to arrive one day early for every time zone you cross. But not all of us can afford the luxury of arriving that early for every race. One way to help overcome jet lag is to have a massage shortly after getting off the plane.

Jitters

Some runners handle pressure better than others. Well trained, they stroll up to the starting line certain that they are about to succeed. Others become very nervous and worry that they won't match their pre-race expectations—or even finish! The best anecdote for pre-race jitters is a successful training program. If you train properly, you should have confidence that you will run well.

Jog Bra

Women formerly wore bras only for support. Lately, bras have become a fashion statement, either peeked at beneath loose clothes or as the only item of upper clothing. Though jog bras may be visible and fashionable, their prime purpose remains support, particularly for big-breasted women who in the past might never have been tempted to take up running.

Jogger

The difference between a jogger and a runner, claimed the late Dr. George Sheehan, is an entry blank.

Jogging

Is there a difference between jogging and running? "Jogging" is generally considered to be "running" done at a slower pace. But it's hard to say at what point running becomes jogging. There is no magic number; it's not a subject that exercise scientists can research in a laboratory. Some very fast runners feel as though they are jogging when they slow down to 6:00 miles. But other runners are at top speed doing a 12:00 mile. Yes, runners! A few easily irritable runners become insulted if someone refers to them as a "jogger." For all practical purposes, there is no difference between jogging and running. Joggers or runners—we are all part of the same breed.

Joy

Running is more than sweat and strained muscles. There is a joy to pursuing fitness and seeking to reach the finish line of a 26-mile 385-yard race that only those who have done it can fully comprehend. Seek to find the joy in running if you want to make it a lifetime pursuit.

Journals

Keeping track of the number of miles you run and how you run them is a good idea. Document your racing as well. If you meet with success or failure, this allows you to check back and determine the reasons. But more than a simple recitation of statistics, your running record should be a journal of your life. Offer a few hints as to how you felt that day, or what else you did around your running. Many years later, like a regular diary, this will allow you to reflect on a happy time of your life.

Journey

The marathon is not a finish line; it is a journey that for some never ends.

Juggling

The order in which you do your workouts is not important as long as you keep all the balls you are juggling in the air. Pick out the two or three key workouts you do each week, get them done, and let everything else fall into place around and between them.

Jump-Start

There is no effective way to jump-start your training, no magic pill for getting you in shape in a hurry. Small increases in the number of miles you run from day to day and week to week work best.

Junk Food

Eating junk food too often will result in junky performances. Proper nutrition during your marathon training is as important as those long runs on the weekends.

Junk Miles

Don't overlook the value of so-called "junk miles." These are slow, extra miles done most often on easy days or in second workouts, sometimes to inflate training mileage to be able to say you ran 40 miles last week instead of only 30. That's not the best idea; nevertheless, don't be shy about including some very slow miles in training, particularly on days between your hard sessions. Junk miles can still do you some good.

Just Do It

What you tell yourself on race day when you arrive at the starting line feeling you're undertrained.

K

is for Kids

Kaleidoscope

Running is like a kaleidoscope. It provides a continually shifting pattern of activities, both in training and in racing. Workouts vary from long runs to short runs to runs in between, done at fast paces and slow paces and even with walking in between. You can run on the roads, through the woods, on the beach or even on 400-meter tracks with soccer games in the infield and participants in other sports all around. You can run in races from 5-K to the marathon, or longer and shorter. This kaleidoscope of running is limited only by your own imagination and willingness to experiment.

Kamikaze

Going out too fast in the first few miles in a marathon is a form of suicide. It's not a matter of *if* you'll crash and burn, it's more a matter of *when*.

Key Workouts

Figure out the key workouts that allow you to succeed with your marathon training. Position those in your workout week, then surround them with various recovery activities that allow you to continue training over a period of time.

The Kick

Increasing your pace and kicking across the finish line is important if you want to look good in your finishing picture and be applauded by spectators. Wait until after you're in the finishing chute to push the button stopping your watch, so you don't get photographed with your head down. You can get your official finishing time later.

Kids

The benefits for children running are so obvious that parents should do everything possible to inspire their children to take up running and other forms of exercise. The link between obesity and other illnesses is strong; cardiovascular disease has been diagnosed even in teenagers. A youngster training for a 5-K is probably going to be less tempted later to experiment with cigarettes or drugs or to hang around with "friends" who climb into a car after downing a six-pack of beer.

Kids Running

Many marathons don't permit children under age 18 to partici-pate, but if you would like your pre-teenage children to become runners, here is how to proceed:

1. **Be a good role model:** The most important thing you can do is enjoy running and express that joy without forcing the issue. Younger kids love to emulate their parents. They'll pick up your positive vibes and want to become runners too.

2. **Make running fun:** If running a marathon to them means long, boring rides in a car and being cooped up in a hotel while Daddy agonizes over his race, they'll be less interested. Find fun family things to do at and around your races.

3. **Run with them:** If you're a half mile ahead of your son or daughter in a 5-K race, they're not going to enjoy it as much as if you run by their side. Don't expect them to train on their own. *You* run *with* them!

4. **Let them set their own pace:** If it's raining and they'd rather play Nintendo instead of doing that 2-mile run *you* have sched-uled for them, relax. Don't push them out the door. Let them de-cide their own level of participation—with guidance, of course.

5. **Don't overtrain or overrace them:** Overtraining doesn't work for you; it won't work for them. Keep distances short. Except for the most gifted, 15 miles a week is a good top limit, and 5-K races are far enough. Marathons are probably too far for most young children, but young children do have a habit of growing up.

Killer Workouts

They may look good in your training diary, but killer workouts just don't work. It may impress your running peers to hear that you ran 20 × 400 meters on the track, but if you have to spend two or three days recovering from that effort, it can have a negative effect on your fitness and even injure you. Steady and consistent training usually works best.

Kilometers

A kilometer is 1,000 meters, 3,280 feet, 0.62 mile. On most outdoor tracks, it is two-and-a-half laps. The marathon is 42.2 kilometers long, which can confuse metrically challenged American runners when they run in international races in which mile markers are not available. But marathons marked in kilometers can provide comfort, particularly in the closing stages. The kilometer markers come back to you much more quickly than do mile markers, thus provide a psychological boost absent from the world in which miles rule.

Kitchens

This frequently used room of the house is usually where we go soon after returning home from our workouts. A quick swig of juice or a snack can serve as a reward for miles run. The kitchen also is a good room in which to record your training miles. Even if you keep a separate diary, post a calendar on the refrigerator or on a wall nearby. Quickly note how many miles you just ran. It can remind you of what you have done and what you need to do.

Knees

There are numerous reasons for sore knees: everything from poor biomechanics to the wrong kind of shoes to overtraining to the plagues of old age. If your knees ache during or after a workout and fail to respond to the classic rehabilitative remedies of icing, elevation, anti-inflammatories and rest, you probably need to see a podiatrist or orthopedist for an informed opinion.

Knowledge

Seek knowledge from those who have run marathons before. And once you have finished, pass on the knowledge you have accumulated to those following in your footsteps. Thus are wisdom and knowledge passed from one to another.

Kooks

There are crazy people all around us who participate in activities that seem strange to us but not to them. Marathon running was considered a strange activity for anyone until it recently became trendy. Appreciate the kooks around you, knowing you are not that far removed from kookiness yourself.

Krispy Kremes

At the convenience store near our condo in Florida where we spend the winters is a kiosk filled with Krispy Kremes, usually baked fresh each morning. I go there most mornings to pick up a newspaper and generally shun the kiosk, practicing self-control in righteous defiance. Nevertheless, every now and then—not more often than once a week—I weaken and purchase a delicacy. For all the running I do, I feel I need occasional treats that break the normal nutritional rules.

L
is for Lifestyle

Lactate Threshold

Untrained runners accumulate lactic acid (see below) sooner than others, at levels as low as 50 to 60 percent of their maximum. Well-trained runners can work at 80 percent without accumulating lactic acid. Speed training can help you raise your lactate threshold, which will allow you to run at a faster pace for a longer period of time and improve your performance.

Lactic Acid

Run at a high rate of speed over a long-enough period and lactic acid eventually will cause you to crash. Here's the reason: Lactic acid is a byproduct of the conversion of glycogen into energy. As long as there is sufficient oxygen flow, lactic acid is flushed from the muscles. As you fall into oxygen debt (in effect, get "out of breath"), lactate begins to accumulate. It is not so much the lactate that causes muscles to fail, but rather the hydrogen released from the lactic acid that inhibits the proper functioning of muscles. This is why quarter-milers struggle as they reach the finish line. But because marathoners run at a gentler pace, they usually do not suffer from a lactic acid buildup. Their slowdown usually is for other reasons. Train properly, pace yourself wisely, and you need not fear lactic acid buildup.

Lactic Acid (myth)

It is a myth that lactic acid causes the sore muscles we feel the day after a hard workout or race. Lactic acid mostly disappears from the system within a half hour after you stop exercising. It is minute tears in the muscles that cause residual soreness.

Layering

The secret to staying warm during winter is layering. As the weather gets colder, begin with a long-sleeved shirt and continue with successive layers of a turtleneck shirt, nylon jacket or parka, or both. Layering gloves will keep your hands warm. Mittens work better than gloves with fingers. Particularly important is a wool cap, since heat escapes upward from the top of the head. Feet usually don't need more than a single pair of socks. Tights will allow your legs to move freely while keeping them warm. Experiment with different layers during workouts, so you know how to dress (usually lighter) for winter races.

Learning

Runners learn from their marathon experiences. They learn about themselves, and they learn about others. They learn how to strengthen their bodies, but they also learn how to strengthen their minds. And often they can apply what they learn in finishing a marathon to other challenges that present themselves in life. In fact, few other activities offer as much of a mind-changing experience as running 26 miles 385 yards for the first time.

Legs

You won't get far without a strong pair of legs. Fortunately, the best exercise for strengthening those legs is running.

Life

Do not let training schedules dictate your life. Let life dictate how you train.

Lifestyle

It's not so much the running that affects your health, but the lifestyle changes that often accompany the decision to run 26 miles 385 yards.

Lifting

Some form of strength training is important for runners—not merely to improve strength and speed, but to improve overall fitness. Women, masters and lightweights probably benefit most. Do your strength training on rest days or when you run easy. Lift *after*, rather than before, you run. Light weights and high repetitions generally work best for runners, because you're less likely to increase bulk (i.e., weight). Work well below your maximum. Beware of squats and heavy lifts that put excessive pressure on your knees. If your muscles are sore more than 24 hours after your strength workouts, you probably are lifting too much. Eliminate strength training entirely in the closing weeks of your marathon mileage buildup.

Lightweight Shoes

Some runners can train or race in lighter shoes than others. This relates usually to how much they weigh and whether or not they possess good biomechanics, what might be called a smooth stride. Coach Jeff Johnson once claimed, "Wear the lightest shoes you can without getting injured." That means in training as well as in racing. Test your lightweight shoes well in workouts before trying them in races, particularly long races. Some runners should never wear lightweight shoes.

Liquids

Drinking liquids while you run is not easy. Unless you take the cup handed to you carefully, you risk spilling much of its contents. Not slowing down and drinking too fast can interfere with your breathing and cause you to gasp. Take too much time at the aid stations, and it will affect your finishing time. If you don't like the liquid offered you, it can nauseate you. Practice drinking during your long runs so that nothing is left to chance in the marathon itself.

Long Runs

If you're training for a marathon, a long run of 10 to 20 miles on the weekend is *de rigueur*. But what if you're training for shorter races? Or what if you're running only for fitness and the good feeling you get from a healthy workout? Do two-hour runs still make sense? Here are some of the reasons they do:

- **Physical benefits:** Regular long runs both maintain and improve your cardiac function. Have a healthy heart and you'll succeed more as a runner—and live longer too.

- **Calorie burn:** You burn more calories by running more miles. The result is what scientists call "cumulative caloric throughput." This allows you to eat more healthy foods and absorb more vitamins and minerals. You need to burn lots of calories to succeed in running, even if at modest intensities.

- **Deficit state:** Only in the long run do you encounter the muscle glycogen depletion that occurs in marathon competition. There are muscle adaptations with long-run training that are difficult to get any other way. When you get into a glycogen-depleted state, you learn to make greater use of fat as an energy source.

- **Focus training:** You have to tune your mind to focus intently on your running for a long period, whether that period is 30 minutes or three hours. That's why long runs are critical to success in any training program, even for a 5-K.

- **Mental boost:** You feel better after you exercise. Everybody who has been running more than a few weeks discovers that.

How far and how often to run long? Mileage probably doesn't matter as much as time. My recommendation would be to program a run of 90 to 120 minutes every other weekend as part of your workout routine.

Limits

There are limits to how hard you can train or how much you improve. Most busy people who seek to become runners never approach these limits.

Listen

Don Kardong, the fourth-place finisher in the 1976 Olympic marathon, suggests that new runners listen to people who have run *lots* of marathons. "They usually know what they're talking about," says Kardong. "And no matter how fit you are, the last few miles are really going to hurt."

Listening

Listen to your body! It knows best, even when your brain does not.

Loading

"Carbo-loading" is a term once used by scientists to describe a pre-marathon regimen in which fast runners did a 20-mile run a week before the race to deplete glycogen (energy) stores, then followed a low-carbohydrate diet for several days before loading up on carbos the last three days. Today's runners, wisely, skip the low-carbohydrate phase and focus on eating lots of carbohydrates as the best way to promote glycogen storage in the muscles.

Logic

There is no logical reason for anyone to run a marathon—which is as good a reason as any to do it!

Long Runs

Do your long runs at a pace 45 to 90 seconds or more slower than your planned marathon pace. Running much faster will *not* get you in better shape and will only increase your risk of injury and the staleness that comes with overtraining. Running your final 20-miler at this deliberately slow pace allows you to run for approximately the length of time it will take you to finish the marathon itself, important for psychological considerations.

Longevity

If you want to have a long running career, determine what activities—both running and activities outside of running—injure you; then avoid them. For some runners, this may mean never doing speedwork or limiting their mileage to a certain level.

Losers

There are few losers in the marathon. Almost everybody who crosses the finish line achieves a victory through the accomplishment of running 26 miles 385 yards. Non-runners who buy into the Vince Lombardi theory that "winning is everything" often can't comprehend this.

Love

Running may seem difficult when you begin. Your legs hurt. Your lungs burn. Muscle soreness lasts for days. New runners ask themselves: How can anything that hurts this much become enjoyable? But as you continue to train over a period of weeks and months, what seemed like an agonizing task will become surprisingly easy. That's when the love affair begins. Come to love running, and you never will want to stop.

Lower Body

Running is a lower-body sport. Your legs are what propel you during a marathon. Upper-body strength is important, but not central, to your success. If you're interested in good health, exercise the total body.

M

is for
Marathon

Magic

There are no magic formulas. Training programs are important in meeting goals, but it's impossible to design a fit-all program to meet everyone's needs. Fatigue, weather, business obligations and family duties all can conspire to prevent your doing what the schedule tells you to run. Sometimes you can juggle workouts to maintain training momentum; other times you simply need to skip the prescribed workout—or do something different. As long as you follow the general pattern of the prescribed training program, you should be able to achieve success.

Make-Up

You can't make up for lost training. If you started late or lost time because of an injury, forget it. Don't double up on your workouts, stealing from your rest days. In the marathon, that may cause you to run slower rather than faster.

Marathon

The marathon is 26 miles 385 yards, or 42.2 kilometers for those who live in the metric world. But it is more than a measured distance along a road. The marathon is also a way of life, a statement, and the measure by which many of us define ourselves.

The Marathon
It's not a race; it's a state of mind.

Massage (before)
The best time for a pre-race massage is the afternoon before a marathon. If you come from out of town, a soothing massage will relieve travel stiffness and invigorate tired muscles. Using your regular massage therapist probably works best, but you probably won't have that option. If using someone new, be *very* precise about instructions. You do not want someone doing deep massage the day before the Big Race. If it hurts, react fast and tell the therapist to back off.

Massage (later)
The best time for a post-race massage is 24 to 48 hours afterward. Free massages at finish-line tents are fine, but swelling and soreness still will continue for several days. Waiting to get home so you can see your regular massage therapist also makes more sense, since he or she knows your body better

and will know where to push, pull and stroke to get you feeling good again.

Massage (necessity)
Obtaining a massage the day before a planned hard workout may loosen you up and allow you to run that workout more efficiently. Obtaining a massage after a particularly hard workout promotes better recovery. Massage therapy is more than a luxury. I schedule a massage every other week as part of my general fitness program, more frequently when training for important races.

Missed Workouts
Unless you are injured, never go two days without running. Even if busy, try to do something that second day. And if you miss that second day, try extra hard to run the third. Or the fourth. Fitness lost is hard to regain. Consistent training can help you achieve success.

Mistakes
Learn from your mistakes; otherwise, you will be destroyed by them.

More

More is both good and bad. More running can get you in fine shape and allow you to achieve Personal Bests in all your performances. But too much "more" and you will injure yourself or become overtrained and fail to achieve your running goals.

Meat vs. Pasta

Just because a meal has meat in it doesn't mean it can't be high in carbohydrates. Potatoes and rice or pasta on the side can keep you on the high side of the carbo-chart.

Memory

Frank Shorter once said, "You can't begin to think about your next marathon until you've forgotten your last one." Even though you're *physically* recovered from your 26-mile effort, you may not be psychologically ready to start training hard again.

Mentor

If you need help getting motivated, turn to fellow runners. Often, they have been there, done that and can help move you along.

Mileage

Increasing mileage is not always easy. It takes months—often years—to double your weekly mileage without crashing. Think of how difficult it is for a beginning runner to go from zero to 25 miles a week. Then consider how much *more* difficult it would be to go from 26 to 50, or from 50 to 100 to reach elite status. Every runner has a perfect training level of weekly miles that will allow him or her to maximize performance and minimize injuries. Finding that level is not always easy to do.

Mindset

Never underestimate yourself. No matter what people say, you can do anything you set your mind to.

Missed Miles

Runners sometimes are forced to skip a workout or two because of illness, injury, competing activities or other reasons. If following a prescribed training program, the temptation is to make up these "missed miles." Unfortunately, the practice of adding miles to future workouts causes more problems than it solves. Don't look back. Continue with your planned training, confident that one or two missed workouts won't matter as long as you maintain your overall consistency.

Morning

Many runners claim the hours around sunrise as their own time. Getting out early in the morning can clear the cobwebs from your head and provide focus for your day. There's something very powerful about rising every morning and getting out on the road before the sedentary segment of humanity starts to stir.

Motivation

Motivation cannot be purchased. It does not come packaged and ready to use. It has to come from within.

Mountains

Training at high altitudes can be challenging for flatlanders, but don't miss an opportunity to run in a scenic location if you visit the mountains. Simply slow your pace, don't be afraid to walk when challenged by a steep hill, and do *not* worry about distance. Determine the approximate length of time it would take you to run your planned workout at sea level, and simply go for that time rather than count mile markers.

Multiple Shoes

If you do much racing, you need more than a single pair of running shoes. It's a good idea to have a newer pair and an older pair, the latter eventually to be retired when you buy a third pair before your most important race, particularly if it's a marathon. Just put enough miles on your new shoes (including one somewhat long run) to ensure that they will not give you problems in the race itself. If you run cross-country or on the track, there are specialty shoes for each different discipline.

Music

Some people can't run unless listening to music. Others (including the Road Runners Club of America) suggest that wearing a radio device can be dangerous because you are less aware of threats—from humans, animals, and machines. It can be impolite if running in a group. And in Big Event races, tuning out by tuning in may distract from the experience of running in front of cheering spectators. The choice is up to the runner, but in some cases you may want to leave your radio at home.

Myself

Running a marathon is a "me" activity, something you do for "myself." It takes extra time to train. It precludes your participation in 5-K's and triathlons and other activities that you like. It forces you to run more miles than maybe you really enjoy. It causes fatigue and sore muscles and requires that you rest more. It takes you away from family obligations and non-running friends. And it can cost money, not only in entry fees, but in travel expenses. But running a marathon can be fulfilling beyond all your expectations, so do it for the myself in you.

N

is for Nutrition

Narcissism

People who work out in health clubs sometimes do so because they want "ripped abs," or "six-packs," or other evidences of muscular development. That's one reason health clubs choose to have mirrors on the walls around the strength machines. After each set of reps, athletes can look in the mirrors and admire how they look. Runners aren't into narcissism. Each mile we run brings its own benefit.

Negative Splits

Run the second half of the marathon faster than the first half (2:01 + 1:59 = 4:00), and you achieve "negative splits." This is a rewarding way to run, since in the closing miles you will pass a lot more runners (many of them walking) than will pass you.

Negative Thoughts

Everybody has bad days and bad workouts, when running gets ugly, when your split times seem unconsciously slow, when you wonder why you ever got talked into training for this stupid marathon. Ho hum. Forget about it. You'll do better the next time you don your shoes. Don't let negative thoughts intrude on your future runs or on the rest of your life, and don't let negative thoughts enter from outside the world of running. Running is the hour each day when you get to think positive.

Nicotine

Smoking and running don't mix. Nicotine not only damages your lungs and raises the risk of cancer, it also affects your cardiovascular system. You'll have trouble breathing if you're a smoker and try to run. Partly for that reason, running can help you kick the nicotine habit. If you want to run a 5-K or finish a marathon, you can definitely improve your performance by throwing that pack of cigarettes away—permanently.

Nipples

Bloody nipples on long runs seem to be more of a problem for males than for women, whose sport bras protect them from friction between skin and singlet. First, avoid cotton. Smoother shirts made out of so-called wicking materials work better. Various products can be used to protect the nipples, including both moisturizers and stick-on pads. You're more likely to find the best products at a running store than at a drugstore.

Pre-marathon Nutrition

Nutrition is an important item for athletes, particularly if you run marathons. Guess wrong on what you eat the last few days and the last few hours before the Big Race, and you may walk, rather than run, the final miles. Here are some recommendations for marathon meals.

- **Seven days out:** As you taper for the race, you'll be cutting miles—but cut calories too. You can afford to gain a few pounds, but don't compensate for your inactivity by overeating. Maintain a training diet high in carbohydrates.

- **24 hours away:** Carbo-loading involves more than what you eat at the pasta party. Think carbohydrates all day long, beginning with breakfast and lunch. And while hydrating, consider juices and sports drinks as well as water. Be cautious what you grab at the free food tables at the Expo.

- **The pasta party:** Spaghetti with marinara sauce is served at most pasta parties, a good choice since marinara offers an extra boost of sodium, which will help maintain your chemical balance the next day. Beware the caffeine, a diuretic, in coffee.

- **Nighttime snack:** Unless late-night eating keeps you awake, top off your energy tank with a few more carbohydrates just before going to bed.

- **Breakfast:** A final fueling about three hours before the start will complete your tank-topping. Wake up early and go back to bed if necessary. But *don't* eat anything that you haven't eaten before in training.

- **The marathon:** Aid stations are plentiful at most major marathons. A combination of water and the available sports drink works best. If you feel you need special foods or fluids, you may need a friend on the course to provide them. Nutrition won't do the job alone. You need to train properly for the race. But eating right before and during the race will help you to a better performance.

Non-running Days

Rest is important for training success, but you don't need to avoid exercise completely. Cross-training can help you recover between yesterday's long run and tomorrow's fast run. Walking, swimming and cycling are all excellent exercises for non-running days. And don't overlook strength training.

Non-running Friends

Your non-running friends don't want to hear your time, or whether or not you set a Personal Record in your first marathon. All they care about is that you finished.

Nordic Skiing

Among sports guaranteed to improve your physical fitness, Nordic (or cross-country) skiing certainly ranks right at the top. Similar to running, Nordic skiing exercises your legs and cardiovascular system, but it also strengthens your upper body. Skiers are the fittest of the fit, having recorded some of the highest oxygen uptake scores. And from a motivational standpoint, if you learn to ski, you no longer will curse snow and cold weather.

Numbers

If you're running your first marathon and expect to finish much slower than four or five hours, you probably should choose a Big City marathon that attracts several thousand or more runners. The larger the field, the more likely you'll have other runners around you in those closing miles when running (or even walking) gets tough. Small marathons can be fun too, but wait until your second or third marathon before trying one.

Numbers (placement)

In road races, numbers go on the front of your singlet, so spectators and officials can identify you as you're coming toward them. Only in track and sometimes in cross-country meets will you be asked to pin the number on your back so that officials can identify you after you've crossed the finish line.

Nutrition

To maintain good nutrition and good health, eat a wide variety of lightly processed foods.

Nutritional Requirements

When you run long distances, your energy requirements increase. For every extra mile you run, you need to add 100 calories to your diet merely to keep your weight in balance. The average runner training for a marathon and running 25 to 30 miles a week probably needs a daily caloric intake near 3,000 to maintain muscle glycogen stores. If you want to lose weight, running will help you with that goal, but you still need to fuel your body with the right kind of food. Carbohydrates work best for endurance athletes.

Nuts

Many non-runners look at us training for marathons and think we're nuts. Okay!

O
is for
Overtraining

Old Runners

At some point, we all begin to slow down. Most runners achieve peak performance between the ages of 20 and 40; after which aging begins to take effect. A few individuals who start running later in life or become smarter about their training can continue to improve into their 50s and even 60s, but aging cannot be postponed forever. Nevertheless, if you run and maintain a healthy lifestyle, you will look and feel a lot better than those who do not.

Old Shoes

Continuing to run in a pair of old shoes after they become worn can be an expensive mistake. You'll save (or at least postpone) the price of a new pair, but you may inevitably pay more (in doctors' fees and time lost) if you become injured because of inadequate foot protection.

Oooooh!

What people say when they see a well-conditioned runner pass. (You think people in passing cars don't notice us?)

Open Roads

There may be clubs you can't join, neighborhoods you can't move into, schools that won't accept you, but the roads are always open.

Order

Most important in any marathon training program are the long runs and rest. The exact order of other workouts is less important. Get your long runs in, coupled with appropriate rest, and you can succeed.

Other Sports

Individuals who participate in other sports while running—particularly while training for a marathon—often set themselves up for an injury. It's because of too much stress. If you want to play racquetball, you probably need to not go for a run that day. If you want to run, you probably need to say "no" to that pickup basketball game. Other sports use different sets of muscles than running and put different stresses on joints. By being in such good shape, runners often can put more stress on undertrained joints and muscles than can the typical untrained weekend warrior. Rather than be less likely to get injured, you may be more likely.

Outside

Running indoors on a treadmill certainly is acceptable behavior if the weather is rotten or if you don't want to run in the dark. But there never will come a time when race directors place treadmills by the starting line of a marathon and offer people a chance to run their 26 miles 385 yards on a moving belt. Get outside as much as you can. You'll see better scenery than you will on the TV screen in your health club.

Office Etiquette

Whether or not your co-workers support your marathoning efforts, you can make office life easier on them, as well as on yourself, if you follow a few suggestions while dealing with the subject of your running

1. **Don't expect everyone to genuflect:** Be subtle in making your marathon plans known. Pinning a training schedule to the wall of your cubicle announces a commitment. If people are interested, they'll ask. You'll soon discover the ones who want to hear more.

2. **Answer questions directly:** Not everybody knows—or cares—that *all* marathons are 26 miles 385 yards long. Most questioners are simply trying to engage you in conversation to show support and interest. Use each question as an opportunity to educate them and others about your plans.

3. **Avoid being self-righteous:** Yes, you've found a new religion, but not everybody desires to be Born Again. Boasting about your New Life inevitably will result in a negative reaction.

4. **Couch potatoes can be sensitive:** That overweight woman in the next cubicle may not want to hear how you've just lost 25 pounds. Your success may be perceived as her failure. Offer sympathy and encouragement only when prompted by another's words and actions.

5. **You're allowed exactly 24 hours of obnoxious behavior:** Wear your finisher's medal to work Monday following the marathon. Claim center stage at the water cooler. Tuesday, put the medal in a drawer. Everybody *loved* what you did, but it's time to return to Real Life.

Overachievement

Achieving success in the marathon requires talent and time to train. But even those of average talent and with limited time can rise above their abilities and achieve extreme levels of success. In perhaps no other event is this more true than in the marathon.

Overeating

Good nutrition is essential during the training buildup to the marathon, but it is particularly important the last three days before the race itself. Carbohydrates rule! But don't overeat, particularly while cruising the aisles at the Expo. Resist eating or drinking free items that may disagree with your stomach.

Overheating

Be particularly cautious about running too fast on hot days, both while training and in races. Realize that you can't run as fast when it's warm. Don't expect to set a Personal Record or maintain your usual training pace, and don't be afraid to bail out early when you're starting to overheat.

Overload

To improve as a runner, you need to gradually overload the system either by running more miles or by running those miles faster. Attempting to do too much of either or both at the same time, however, can cause you to become overtrained or injured. Finding the right overload dosage is the most difficult task for any coach or runner.

Overstriding

Theoretically, the longer your stride, the faster you should be able to run. A stride four feet long covers more ground than one three feet long. But everybody has a stride length that is perfect for his or her size and strength. A long stride causes the runner to lose momentum and waste energy by pushing too far ahead of his center of gravity. If you overstride, you may lose efficiency and find yourself running slower rather than faster. But understriding can also limit your efficiency and speed.

Overtraining

You need to train hard to get in shape to run 26 miles, but excessive training may leave you exhausted and cause you to perform worse, not better. Warning signs include dead legs, sore muscles, an elevated pulse rate on rising and an inability to sleep soundly despite being tired. Take a day or two off to rest, and, while doing so, reevaluate your training plan.

Overweight

To a certain point, the less you weigh, the faster you can run. Excessive weight can limit your performance, since carrying an extra 10 pounds in love handles is the same as carrying a 10-pound pack on your back. The best way to lose weight is to combine diet and exercise: eating less and running more. But don't go on a crash diet, since losing weight too rapidly is bad for your health. And be sure to determine what weight is best for your build and body frame. Too little weight can slow you down too.

Oxygen

Muscles operate efficiently only if supplied with large quantities of oxygen. When your heart muscle becomes stronger and your cardiovascular system operates more efficiently, you will be able to run faster. Training causes this to happen. Training also results in increased blood flow through the muscle fibers and improvement of the fibers themselves—all of which improves your ability to use oxygen.

P

is for Pace

Pace

In any training schedule, "pace" refers to the speed at which you plan to run the race you are training for. For instance, if you're planning to run a 3:45 marathon, your race pace would be 8:35 miles. If you were training for a 5-K or a 10-K, your pace would be faster. It's usually a good idea to do at least some of your training at race pace, so you accustom your muscles to running at that particular speed.

Pacing Error

Running at a pace a few seconds too fast at the beginning of a marathon can cost you minutes over the last miles and even make it impossible to finish.

Pacing Teams

Since being started in 1995 by Amby Burfoot at the St. George Marathon to help runners qualify for the 100th Boston Marathon, the *Runner's World* pacing teams have proved enormously popular. Other marathons such as Chicago and Columbus now provide their own pacing teams made up of experienced runners leading others through evenly paced races at times from three to five hours or more. The theory is that, if you can maintain a steady pace throughout, you will be less likely to "hit the wall" at 20 miles. Spreading your energy over the full 26 miles makes sense. If the marathon you choose doesn't offer pacing teams, consider recruiting a friend for support. Following the pace of others, however, can be risky if you don't know how fast they plan to finish.

Pain (1)

Beginners often suffer more pain than experienced runners, because their untrained muscles react to the stress of exercise. Running does hurt at first. But, if beginners persist, they eventually become experienced runners and learn to accept a certain amount of discomfort so that they can reap the benefits of improved fitness.

Pain (2)

Pain is the body's signal to slow down—or stop entirely! If you feel pain at the beginning of a run and it diminishes as you continue, take that as a sign to keep going. But if the pain gets worse, you'll be making a mistake if you try to push through the pain. Stop. Walk. Take a taxi home, if possible. If ice and anti-inflammatory medication fail to cause the pain to diminish after two or three days of rest, you should definitely make an appointment with a sports-medicine specialist to find out what's wrong.

Parenting Runners

Children—like adults—differ in their ability to absorb training. Some genetically gifted youngsters seem to have the ability to float across the ground and run forever. Others may need closer parental supervision. Dr. Jordan Metzl (who has run 13 marathons, Boston seven times) says this is particularly true at puberty: between 8 and 12 for girls and 10 and 14 for boys. "There is some risk that *excessive* running can damage the growth plates," he says. "As to what is 'excessive,' there's no research that would provide us with an exact number. I'm comfortable with children running distances up to 5-K and 10-K if they're properly trained. I'm not a believer in kids under 18 running marathons, and those under 14 should probably stay on the low side of 13 miles."

Patience

In this era of instant gratification, people want their pleasures—*now!* That may work in some areas of life, but not if you suddenly decide to run a marathon. Be patient. Some individuals can finish a marathon after a few months of running; most cannot. If you are new to the sport, consider your current physical fitness before sending in your entry blank. Building a good base with short workouts over an extended period makes marathon training easier once you do start. It takes time (and intelligence) to get in shape. Waiting until next year could be the smartest decision you make.

Perception

What makes a running course difficult? It is partly your own perception. Inadequate training can make even the easiest courses tough to run. I remember running the Blueberry Stomp, a 15-K in Plymouth, Indiana, one year when I was in peak shape. I had won a gold medal at the World Masters Championships several weeks before. The course seemed flat as an ironing board, and I ran 45 minutes and change. The following year, less dedicated, I returned to the same race far from peak form and ran several minutes slower. I thought, "Where were all those hills last year?"

Perfection

Don't expect every workout to be perfect, particularly if you are running long. You might feel great one week doing a 12-miler, then struggle the next going 10. It may not be your training. Other factors can contribute to make a run less than perfect: too little sleep, too much stress at work, a virus you caught or are about to catch. Simply continue, knowing that your next workout probably will feel much better.

Performance

Some runners judge performance by whether they won or not. Others define success or failure by how fast they ran, whether or not they matched their time expectations. Still others judge performance by how good they felt running, focusing on the experience. Only *you* can judge your performance. Avoid letting others sit in judgment of you.

Periodization

The best training programs involve some form of "periodization," the idea being that there are different periods of the year for different types of training. Speed training usually is best accomplished during warm summer months. Cold winter breezes may force you to ease back on the miles and do some strength training indoors. Cool periods between those two seasons are the best times to compete if you're a long-distance runner. Your choice of races and dates will dictate the type of training you do and when you do it. Periodization not only alleviates boredom; it allows you to maximize your athletic potential.

Play

Running should be "play," claimed the late Dr. George Sheehan. "In play you realize simultaneously the supreme importance and utter insignificance of what you are doing. You accept the paradox of pursuing what is at once essential and inconsequential. In play you can totally commit yourself to a goal that minutes later is completely forgotten."

Position

Starting in the back of the pack in large races is a good strategy for first-timers. You won't have to worry about starting too fast. With thousands ahead, you will take several minutes to cross the starting line and may lose more time before you can reach peak pace. Don't panic. Your focus as a first-time marathoner should be to finish, not finish fast. Since most of the major races today are timed with the ChampionChip, you won't lose any time, since you will be timed from the moment you cross the starting line, not when the gun sounds.

Power

Power equals speed. Speed equals power. If you can improve your strength by doing supplemental exercises such as weight lifting, you should be able to become a better runner.

Predictions

One handy prediction formula for determining how fast you can run a marathon is to multiply your most recent 10-K time by 4.66. That's if you're in great shape and have done the endurance training. A more reasonable formula is to multiply your 10-K time by 5.0. Still another formula is to double your half-marathon time and add 10 minutes. Various prediction charts exist in books and on the Internet. But at some point, you need to step out on the course and see exactly how fast you can run 26 miles 385 yards.

Pre-race Workout

My approach to the last three days before an important race is to do no running two of the days and run only a few miles on the third. I prefer doing this pre-race workout the day before. It's partly to loosen my legs (particularly if I've had to travel) and partly to reduce nervousness. I jog about a mile to some grassy area and do two to three easy "strides," 100 meters or so near race pace. That gets me ready to run the next day.

Pride

The pride in finishing a marathon is much greater than all the pain endured during the marathon.

Prize

St. Paul once said, "Do you not know that those who run in a race, all indeed run, but only one receives the prize? So run as to obtain it." That message might have been true 20 centuries ago, but if St. Paul could experience today's mass-participation marathons, he would agree that more than one runner benefits from the race. Regardless of whether you expect to win a prize, take St. Paul's advice and run so as to obtain it.

Priorities

Some runners race too frequently: as often as every weekend in short-distance races such as the 5-K and 10-K. Racing can be fun and can become an important part of your social life, but races also can detract from your training, particularly while getting ready for an important marathon. Too-frequent racing also can cause injuries. At some point, you need to back off and consider your priorities related to both training and racing and to other demands on your time. Once you do that, you can determine how often to go to the starting line.

Promises, Promises

Never promise your spouse before your first marathon that this will be the only time.

Pulse

Taking your pulse is an effective way to measure your stress level during workouts and in marathons. Heart-rate monitors will do that job for you, but it's easy to simply put a finger on a vein and count. If your pulse is elevated above the norm for the activity you're doing, that is a hint that you may be pushing it too hard. Measuring pulse rate before you get up in the morning allows you to monitor whether you are overtrained or not.

Pushing

One way to improve is to add a new element to your program. For most new runners who began by doing progressively longer runs, this element is often speedwork. Don't be shocked by how "slow" you are at the start of your speed program. Continue to push gently against the edge of the envelope, and you should improve.

Q

is for Quality

The Quads

The most important muscles in running are the calf muscles, below the knees. They come into action as your foot is on the ground, propelling you forward. But the quadricep muscles above and in front of the knee are important too, since they lift the foot off the ground during each stride. It is often the quads that go toward the end of marathons, reducing runners to a slow shuffle. To strengthen the quads, run hills, do half-squats or lunges, and cross-train on a bicycle.

Qualifying (for Boston)

The Boston Marathon welcomes only the best marathoners to its starting line in suburban Hopkinton each April. To qualify for the race, male runners 18 to 34 must run a marathon in 3:10; women runners in the same age group qualify by running 3:40. Standards for older runners increase by five minutes every five years. (For example, men 35 to 39 qualify by running 3:15.) To run in Boston is to achieve a standard well respected by your running peers—but doing so requires talent, training and time.

Quality

When trying to improve or maintain performance, focus less on quantity and more on quality. Running more miles doesn't always work if they are slower miles. You can train successfully on three workouts a week as long as you maintain quality.

Quality (choices)

Not everybody has the time or inclination to train seven days a week. And even if so inclined, you may risk injury if you fail to program regular rest days into your schedule. In planning your training—regardless of the race distance it's for—focus on the quality workouts and eliminate some of the quantity workouts (i.e., eliminate easy days that mainly give you extra mileage). Long runs on the weekend are still essential if you want to call yourself a marathoner. Regardless of the speed at which you run it, a 20-miler still qualifies as a quality workout.

Quality (life)

Kenneth H. Cooper, M.D., suggests that a healthy lifestyle that includes appropriate amounts of exercise can add six to nine years to your life and—most important—contribute greatly to the quality of that life.

Quantity

To maintain fitness, lose weight or train for a marathon, the quantity of your running may be almost as important as quality. You need to run a certain number of miles, and often it doesn't matter how fast you run them as long as you maintain consistency in your workouts. Generally speaking, 10 to 15 miles a week of running will get you in good shape. For racing at the 5-K and 10-K level, you may need to ratchet your weekly miles up to 20 or 25. For marathons, 40 to 50 miles may be necessary to ensure a comfortable finish. Elite runners—those who finish in the front of the pack—often run twice a day and log 100 or more miles a week.

Quantifying Quality

The number of miles you run each week may not reflect the quality of your workouts or even the quantity. A run in hot weather or at high altitude may result in more stress and, in some respects, a "better" workout than the numbers suggest. One way to quantify workouts is by wearing a heart-rate monitor. By checking your pulse rate, you can determine just how hard you are running.

Quarters

The 400-meter (quarter-mile) is the most frequently run distance by runners doing interval training on a track. A "quarter" is one lap on most outdoor tracks; thus, its convenience in a speed workout. You run one quarter fast, then jog or walk another quarter slow, then repeat the fast quarter. A typical interval workout would be 10 × 400 meters, jogging or walking between repeats. This is a very effective way to build speed.

Questions

If puzzled by some aspect of your training or the running sport, don't hesitate to ask. Most other runners have been there and done that. Most are happy to share with you what they have learned.

Quickness

Being fast in the first step is important if you're a sprinter running the 100 meters or a basketball player who needs to drive around the person guarding you. But quickness can be a curse in the marathon. It's those slow steps—lots of them—that get you to the finish line.

Quiet

For those who work or live in a busy and noisy business or family environment, time spent running may be the only quiet time they have during the day. But some running areas offer more silence than others. In seeking a break from your normally hectic routine, go for long runs in the woods. You may see other runners, but you also may encounter deer. And deer don't do much talking.

Quitting

Dropping out of a marathon can be a very disappointing experience, particularly if you have trained 18 weeks or more for the event. By quitting, you may feel that you brand yourself a failure. But if you're undertrained or injured or overheated on a very hot day, dropping out may be the better part of valor. Suck in your disappointment and look forward to doing better the next time.

Quotas

With the current popularity of marathoning, many races have had to establish quota systems to limit the number of entrants. This often is necessary to avoid crowding the field. Some marathons (Chicago, Grandma's) issue numbers to the first who enter. Others (New York, London) use a lottery to determine entrants. To qualify for Boston, runners need to meet time standards related to age and gender. If you want to run a specific marathon, obtain an entry form early to make sure you understand how to get in.

R

is for Roadkill

Race Day

Don't do anything on race day that you haven't done in training, particularly during the long runs. Don't wear new shoes that you haven't trained in before. Don't wear shorts and singlet that you might have bought the day before at the Expo. Don't eat or drink anything different from what you've eaten or drunk before or during your training runs. Don't, don't, don't, if you want to do.

Racing

Running occasional races at distances other than the marathon will allow you to test your fitness level and also to predict how fast you can run at longer distances. Doing this will allow you to gauge better your race pace. A certain amount of racing will strengthen your legs and fine-tune your speed. Too much racing, however, may rob time from your training and cause excessive fatigue.

Radios

Among the subdivisions in running are those who run without radios and those who run with. It's like the difference between sailboaters and power boaters. The former like to float with the wind, appreciative of the silence provided by their motorless environment. The latter respond more to excitement and don't mind the noise as long as it gets them where they're going.

Rain

For sensual pleasure during a workout, nothing beats running in a warm summer rain. It beats running under a hot sun with temperatures soaring into the 90s any day. Soaked shoes, however, are not fun. Try to pick courses where the water doesn't accumulate in deep puddles.

Real Life

Running is not Real Life. Work, family and all the things that surround running are Real Life. For some, running allows them to escape Real Life. For others, running allows them to expand upon Real Life.

Reason

Marathons feature the triumph of desire over reason.

Rebuild

The reason for hard training is to break the body down so that it can be rebuilt stronger than before. Only when you fail to allow the body time to rebuild do you risk injury.

Recovery

Take your time recovering after races, particularly after marathons. Coming back too soon can cause illness or injury. One rule of thumb suggests a day of rest or easy running for every mile run in a race (26 rest days after a marathon). Another suggests one for every kilometer (42 after a marathon). Rules of thumb don't always work for everybody, however, so listening to your own body signals before resuming hard training is more important. Often, the determining factor is not how quickly your body recovers but how quickly your mind recovers, since you temporarily will have lost your main training goal.

Redux

Many track athletes discover that the marathon is a much tougher event than they previously have encountered. It takes more miles of training and a specific type of training.

Then race day arrives, and suddenly it is over and you have to start training again for the next one.

Red Flag

Bob Williams, a coach in Portland, Oregon, claims that runners must pay attention to red flags. He warns: "If you begin to feel symptoms of an injury during or after a training session—no matter how slight—the red flag goes up." Williams recommends immediate icing to stop inflammation. If, the next day, you are still sore, then you need to take 72 hours off. "Pain is your red flag," says Williams. "You can only complicate an injury by running on it."

Red Line

Every runner has a point, a red line on his tachometer, beyond which he dare not pass without risking illness or an injury. Most often, red lines are related to miles run in training, either weekly or in single sessions. But weather, nutrition and outside activities also can influence where your red line lies. Smart training and intelligent use of rest sometimes will permit you to nudge your red line upward and run faster. Otherwise, you usually will achieve the most success (and avoid injuries) if you train well beneath that red line.

Reflection

Reflecting back on a running career that has spanned more than a half century, I realize that with the knowledge I now possess, I could have trained more intelligently and raced more successfully, running not only faster times but winning more races. But would this have made me a better person? I'm not sure it would have. I am what I am as much because of my defeats as my victories, and I don't want to rewrite history. Still, if I had only known then. . . .

Registration

As running becomes more and more popular, many races have begun to limit the number of entries. In order to assure yourself a place in the field, you may need to register months in advance. The down side on this is that if you later decide not to run, or become injured, you lose your money. The *up* side is that once you send that money, you signal your commitment. It is always easier to focus your training and motivate yourself with an end goal in sight.

Regrets

Running a marathon is a good way to cancel many of the "regrets" people carry with them: the fact that they never enrolled in medical school, or invested in that can't-miss-stock, or let that sensitive guy or gal slip out of their lives. Running a marathon signifies a commitment, and once you cross that finish line (regardless of time), nobody can take the achievement away from you.

Relaxation

The most important benefit from massage may not be muscle recovery, but rather the relaxation effect. A relaxed muscle is much less likely to get injured.

Repeats

Here is how to run a "repeat," sometimes referred to as a "rep." Run fast for a distance or period of time; then rest. Repeat the distance. A typical repeat workout would be 3 × mile with five minutes' walking between. Running repeats on a track, or even on the road, is an effective form of speedwork.

Reverse Splits

Running the second half of the marathon faster than the first half is called achieving "reverse splits." (Your late-mile splits are faster than your early-mile splits.) This is an effective strategy for elite runners, who sometimes sit and wait until one or more runners increase the pace to break away and finish fast. Elite runners usually don't care how fast they run as long as they win. It is much more difficult for runners back in the pack to achieve a fast time using the reverse split strategy. A steady pace throughout usually results in a better performance.

Review

One reason to keep a running diary is so that you can review what worked well and what went wrong with your training. If you set a Personal Record, you'll want to know what training produced that success. If you crashed and burned, reviewing your diary may offer some hints as to mistakes you will not want to repeat.

Revving

Beware training too hard. If you consistently rev your engine faster and faster, it will explode.

Rigor Mortis

Runners who go out too fast—particularly in the marathon—begin to suffer what passes as rigor mortis in the closing miles. This is also known as getting the "riggies," the moment when the bear jumps on your back or seeks to devour you. You have hit the wall! Regardless of the name given this occurrence, the closing miles are not going to feel comfortable. Prudent pacing is the way to avoid rigor mortis.

Recovery Mode

There is no exact formula for marathon recovery, but here are some recovery tips to help you feel better faster:

1. **Recovery starts in the finishing chute.** Keep moving. Keep drinking. Start eating. Your body wants to be fed.

2. **Run no more.** Your body also needs rest. No running for the next 72 hours and very little the rest of the week.

3. **Forget cross-training.** Sure, you could cycle or swim, but that will only delay the recovery process.

4. **Schedule a massage.** More than pampering, massage will soothe those tired muscles.

5. Look after your body. If you have any problems, see a sports doctor. Don't wait two weeks to fix that black toenail.

Within a week, most muscle soreness should be gone. But don't rush. Your body may feel better, but it's still in recovery mode.

Risk

Increasing mileage or adding speedwork—or doing both—in an effort to improve performance is risky. You could crash and burn, either while training or in the race itself. You may become injured; you may become overtrained. Still, sometimes it's worth taking a risk to set a Personal Record or qualify for Boston. You can limit your risks by making only small shifts. Increase mileage gradually. Limit speed sessions until you become accustomed to the rhythm of fast running. You may surprise yourself by achieving a new level of success.

Roadkill

Traffic laws apply to runners as well as to automobiles, particularly when runners share the roads with those automobiles. To avoid being roadkill, run facing traffic so that you can see what's coming at you. Don't hesitate to move onto the shoulder rather than assume the driver will yield to you, or even see you. On cross-training days while on a bicycle, be especially cautious and ride with—not against—traffic. You don't want to become a hood ornament on somebody's S.U.V.

Rookies

It's easy to spot a rookie runner, someone who has just taken up the sport or maybe decided to run a few miles as a respite from his or her regular sport. Rookie runners often run on the right (which is wrong) side of the road, with traffic coming from behind them. After they have run a few times in areas populated by regular runners, they realize that everybody else is running on the left side, facing traffic. They move over and cease being rookies. (See Roadkill, above.)

Rotating

One pair of shoes is simply not enough if you consider yourself a serious runner, one who trains more than occasionally. You need at least two or three pairs so that you do not run in the same shoes day after day. Any time you run, sweat drains into your shoes, and the protective materials become compressed. Rotating shoes allows them to dry out and re-bound between workouts.

Rules

Don't run more than one marathon a year. Don't run too much, too often, too far, too soon or even too little! Don't forget to stretch. Don't run more than three hours. Don't forget to walk. Don't forget to drink. Don't wear a radio when you run. Rules, including many laid down in this book, can both make you a more successful runner and inhibit how you run.

Ruts

It's good to be regular with your training, but you also can get in a rut if you train at the same time, at the same speed, doing the same distance. Feel free to experiment with different routines to bring more variety to your training and your life.

S

is for Schedules

Scenery

If you find yourself in a rut—running on the same course, for the same distance, at the same speed, day after day—and running becomes a grind, consider taking a short (or long) trip to an area of scenic beauty. *Runner's World* refers to these as "Rave Runs." A run along a bucolic stream or on the trails of a state park may be all you need to revive your interest in running. And when planning a vacation to a scenic spot, don't forget your running shoes.

Schedules

Training schedules aren't carved in concrete. When following any coach's training program, adapt it to your own schedule of work and family obligations. But make sure you maintain the pattern of the training schedule you follow; otherwise, there's no sense selecting it.

72 Hours

If you injure yourself during a workout and still feel pain the next day, your immediate response should be to rest 72 hours. Pain is your signal to stop, particularly if the pain gets worse as you continue to run. Forget what your training program says to do that day. You don't want to complicate the injury by running on it, or even by cross-training. Icing the injury and taking an anti-inflammatory may provide some relief, but if after 72 hours it still hurts when you run, you probably need to see a sports doctor for an evaluation.

Sex

Running can make you a better lover. Not only will you become more attractive to members of the opposite sex if you are physically fit, but your performance should improve in more ways than 5-K times. There is some truth to the saying that long-distance runners can keep it up longer. However, probably not the night after a marathon or hard workout, when you may prefer to roll over and go to sleep.

Shinsplints

Doctors claim that the term "shinsplints" is misleading and covers four or five different injuries. They prefer "medial tibial pain syndrome." Regardless of name, it hurts when you've got it. Shinsplints most often is a problem encountered by beginners and runners who make a sudden increase in mileage. Muscle and foot imbalances and extra weight (as well as poor shoe choice) can add to the problem. Icing, anti-inflammatories and rest can help repair the damage. The best preventative is a well-designed and gradual training program.

Shoelaces

Here's how to keep your shoelaces tied without double-knotting them. Todd Henderlong of Opportunity Enterprises in Valparaiso, Indiana, offers the following advice: "Tie your shoes like you normally would, but when you get to the part when you make the first bow, rather than wrap the lace around the base of that bow once, wrap it around *twice*. Then pull the second bow through, making sure the second bow goes under both wraps. Looking at the finished product, rather than having two bows and two ends with one wrap, you'll have two bows and two ends being held together by two wraps." To undo the knot, simply pull both single ends and untie them like you normally would. It's much faster than untying double-knotted shoes. Henderlong guarantees that your shoelaces will never come untied if you follow this advice.

Shoes

Runners training regularly probably need at least two or more pairs of shoes, alternating from day to day. And they don't necessarily have to be the same brand and model. Try different models. Experiment. If you find something that works, keep it. As for your racing shoes, you don't want too many miles on them, particularly for a marathon, but you need to run in them enough to determine whether or not they are going to cause you any problems.

Short Stride

A short stride is usually more economical than a long stride for distance runners. More important for maintaining speed is stride *cadence* rather than stride length. A lot of quick steps will get you to the finish line faster.

Sick Days

It's not uncommon to get sick and miss workouts during peak training. Research even suggests that high-intensity training can temporarily damage your immune system and make you more likely to get a cold or the flu. If you do miss a few workouts, don't worry—and don't feel you need to "make miles up." If you train consistently over a period of weeks, months and even years, occasional lapses are not a problem. More of a problem is trying to come back too soon after a cold (and especially after the flu).

Singing

Running should be like singing. You sing because you feel happy—and want to stay happy. You don't sing because someone forced you to do it.

Sleep

Sleeplessness before a marathon is normal among runners who race. It's mainly nervousness. And if you've tapered properly by cutting back on training mileage, withdrawal symptoms can compound the problem. Nevertheless, even while lying in bed with your eyes wide open, you're still resting your muscles. It's the night before the night before that counts. Staying off your feet much of the last 24 hours before the marathon will get you to the starting line ready to perform regardless of how many Z's you got.

Sleep Loss

Sleep loss is progressive. You can shortchange sleep for days, even weeks, but sooner or later it will catch up with you. The result may be injury, illness or simply an overall tired feeling that will prevent your enjoying your running. When this happens, you need to take time off from running and/or other activities crowding your schedule.

Slow

The adjective "slow" does not exist when it comes to running. All runners are "fast," no matter at what speed they run.

Sloth

People who are not runners believe that the reward for all the miles we run will be crippling knee pain when we get older. In addition, running gets you sweaty and hurts and wastes a lot of time that could be used much more profitably, such as eating bonbons and watching situation comedies on TV.

Don't listen to "friends" who criticize your commitment to running.

Slowdown

Slowing down at the end of a race can be frustrating. You're moving well, headed for a Personal Record, then suddenly: *Boom!* You stagger home. Reverse splits are the ideal, but they're not practicable for everybody. Some people have more fast- than slow-twitch muscles and therefore face inevitable slowdowns. Training may be part of the answer: more long runs spread out through the year. Or pick a pacing plan that compensates for the slowdown, such as running faster in the middle (though not at the start) of the race. Regardless of what happens, finish with honor—even though your time is slower than anticipated.

Smartness

Smart training is more important than hard training.

Smoking

There is no question that cigarette smoking inhibits performance. Although people are born with excess lung capacity, smoking certainly interferes with your ability to transport oxygen to the muscles. More important, smoking interferes with your ability to live longer. A lot of people find that when they substitute a positive addiction (running) for their negative addiction (smoking), it becomes easier to give up the latter.

Socks

Socks are an important, but oft-forgotten, item of running apparel. Pick the wrong socks and you are more likely to experience blisters. Try to avoid cotton socks, particularly when you run longer than 30 minutes. Cotton holds water and bunches up under your feet. Instead, select thin and tight socks made from a moisture-wicking material. The tight fit will prevent your socks' bunching, and the material will wick away the moisture and help you avoid sliding around in your shoes and causing blisters.

Speedwork

Any training done at race pace or faster would be considered "speedwork," regardless of whether your planned race is the 800 or the marathon. But choose your pace carefully. A common beginner's mistake is to run speedwork flat out—beyond race pace. While a certain amount of flat-out training can contribute to your fitness level, too much of it can increase your risk of injuries.

Speedwork (benefits)

Some forms of speedwork are best for improving strength; others, for improving endurance. Some help you with your form; others, with your concentration. Another important consideration is the confidence that comes from training hard in a measured environment. How you do your speedwork may depend on your specific situation and surroundings. Your training plans will be dictated by whether you live near a track, a golf course, or a wooded area with trails. Weather conditions may be a factor, as will be the length and importance of the race for which you're training. But the one thing certain about speedwork is that it works. Speedwork can make you a faster runner.

Speedwork (deficits)

Doing speedwork too often can be a detriment if you're training for a marathon, particularly if you're not used to this form of fast training. As the miles increase, speedwork may provide just that extra dosage of stress that pushes you off the edge. Unless you're an expert runner, the best time to do speedwork is outside the training period for the marathon.

Sprints

Running as fast as you can for a very short distance is called a "sprint." Repeating this several times during a training session is called doing "sprints." A typical sprint workout is 6 × 100 meters at full speed, walking until rested between. You can improve your speed and form doing sprints, but this form of speedwork must be embraced carefully because of the risk of injury.

Steadiness

Slow and steady wins the marathon race. Fast first miles will result in fades near the finish. An even pace is the most efficient way to run the marathon. Surging—unless you are a lead runner testing your opponents—wastes energy. And maybe it's not that good an idea for the front-runners either. Steadiness also pays dividends in training.

Stopping Short

Using a marathon as a training run is a good idea—as long as you don't go the entire distance. Drop out at 13, 16 or 20 miles, depending on how easy it is to catch a ride back to the start or finish. The main advantage of doing long runs in races is that you can enjoy the spirit of the event, the fact that the streets are closed to traffic, and the aid tables. If you *do* employ this strategy, however, you should register for the race and not run as a bandit.

Storing Glycogen

When it comes to fueling your body for a marathon, the amount of glycogen you can store depends on a number of factors, claims *Runner's World* diet columnist Liz Applegate. "Glycogen storage is a function of training and fitness," she explains. "With increased levels of fitness for endurance activities, your ability to store glycogen is greatly improved."

Strength

Even when you have gone as far as you can and everything hurts, and you are staring at the specter of self-doubt, you can find a bit more strength deep inside if you look closely enough.

Stress

Part of the training process for the marathon is the psychological ability to continue to perform under high stress: in effect, to push on through the pain barrier. Gradually increasing the length of your longest runs will help you overcome the mental barriers that are part of finishing a marathon.

Stress Fractures

All fractures heal differently. Although a knowledgeable physician can offer an educated guess as to how soon you can return to running, it is, at best, just that: a *guess*. Don't risk a relapse by returning too quickly. Before resuming running, try to determine the cause of the stress fracture: too much mileage? an uneven gait? insufficient stretching? If you can learn from your injury, you may be able to avoid a next one.

Stress Fractures (Diagnosis)

Stress fractures often are difficult to diagnose—even with X-rays. The problem is that stress fractures don't show up on

X-rays immediately. Only if calcification develops as the bone begins to heal can doctors confirm that the pain you feel is a legitimate stress fracture.

Stretching

Stretching your muscles before, during and after you run can provide an effective dose of prevention against injuries—and can be used to cure injuries, if done properly. But stretching too hard or too long can actually *cause* injuries, and it certainly can waste time that you'd rather spend running. So stretch like a cat. Be lazy about it, stretching often for short periods at odd hours of the day, even while sitting at a desk or riding in a car. Find the two or three stretches that work best for you and do them when you want to get and stay loose.

Strides

Strides are the same as Sprints (above), but at a slower, controlled pace. A typical workout featuring strides is 6 × 100 meters at 10-K or marathon pace. You can improve your form by doing occasional strides as part of your warm-up or cooldown before a speed workout or race.

Stubbornness

Sometimes runners can get into trouble if they stubbornly follow a training plan and run when injured or fatigued. Bad things may follow: an injury or an inability to perform up to expectations. But it is also stubbornness that pushes us out the door every day into an activity that we love and that will provide us with both fun and good health.

Stupidity

If you want to run fast and remain uninjured, try to avoid doing really dumb things in your training.

Support

Sometimes marathoners think that they can do everything on their own, but support from others is essential, everyone from volunteers and spectators along the course to a helpful spouse who minds the kids while you train.

Surface

All the experts claim that asphalt is softer than concrete for your training needs, but in all honesty the difference is not that great. If forced to make a choice between these two surfaces, pick the course that's most appealing on that particular day. But choose other surfaces too—trails, tracks, grass, beaches. If you want to call yourself a Complete Runner, you need to learn to run everywhere.

Surprises

Even though all the training runs go perfectly, it does not mean that the marathon will go the same or that you won't be faced with an unexpected challenge. The weather can change. A blister may form. A cold may occur. That friend you expected to hand you jelly beans at 20 miles may fail to appear. Prepare for surprises; that way you never can be surprised.

T

is for Training

Take Time

Building a good base with short workouts over an extended period makes training easier once you do start your marathon buildup. It takes time to get in shape. Take it!

Taper

In the taper before an important marathon, you're not training the muscles; you're resting the muscles. It's a time in your training when rest is usually best. David L. Costill, Ph.D., of Ball State University, did extensive research on resting swimmers and found that proper tapering could take chunks off their times. Most of the swimmers were training harder than necessary and were tearing themselves down.

Tedium

Running the same course and the same distance at the same pace day after day can become tedious. To keep running exciting, you need variety.

Tempo Runs

Tempo runs are best defined by time rather than distance. Begin by jogging until warmed up, then very gradually accelerate until you are running near 10-K pace, hold that pace for a period, then gradually decelerate until you're jogging again. A 30-minute tempo run might consist of 5 to 10 minutes of jogging, then a gradual acceleration for 5 to 10 minutes to 5 minutes of peak speed followed by 5 to 10 minutes of slowing down. Transitions should be smooth, determined by how you feel rather than by a preset plan.

The Three Goals

There are three goals in a marathon: (1) to finish, (2) to improve and (3) to win. The goal you strive for depends upon the level at which you are running.

Throwaway

The best race conditions are those in which you're actually cold at the starting line. So fight the freeze with throwaway clothes. If you don't have a friend who can take your warm-up sweats at the last minute, bring some old clothes you can dump when the gun sounds. And maybe an old long-sleeved or ugly T-shirt that you can jauntily throw to the crowd once your blood starts flowing. If temperatures start to rise, you'll be glad you didn't overdress.

Starting to Train

Whether you are a novice hoping to finish your first marathon or an experienced veteran seeking a Personal Record, here is a checklist to consider as you start to train:

1. **Assess your fitness level:** What sort of shape are you in? How long have you been running? The better your background, the better your chances of success.

2. **Determine time available:** Training for a marathon not only requires energy, it also requires a time commitment, particularly as the mileage increases toward the end. Do you have, or can you make, time?

3. **Gear up:** The most important item of equipment is your running shoes. Treat yourself to a new pair now to make sure you are well shod for all the miles you plan to run.

4. **Define your goal:** If you've chosen a specific marathon to run, half of your goal is set. But how fast do you want to run? Or will you be happy finishing regardless of time?

5. **Announce your intent:** Don't keep your plans a secret. Tell friends and family that you intend to run a marathon. They will become an important support group to keep you on track during training and the marathon itself.

6. **Plan your time:** When is the best time of day to run? Where are the best areas to train? Don't leave to chance these important decisions.

7. **Find a support group:** The long runs can be achieved much more easily if you can run with others. Join a class, but if you can find even *one* other runner to train with, it will make your task much easier.

8. **Program rest:** When it comes to marathon training, more isn't always better. The most important days on your schedule are those on which you rest or run easy. This permits you to run harder on the tough days.

9. **Learn to eat:** Nutrition is critical to marathon success, not only in the race itself but also during the weeks and months of training. You need a well-balanced diet high in carbohydrates. Avoid fad diets!

10. **Carry through:** Don't let your commitment go to waste. Don't become diverted by other goals. Whether your goal is to finish your first marathon or improve a Personal Record, you will succeed only if you focus your attention on success.

Time of Day

Regardless of whether you are a morning person or an evening person, run at the time of day that is most convenient for you and for those around you. The availability of daylight also may be a factor, particularly in the winter. Eventually, you will determine the workout time that is most convenient.

Time Training

While training for a marathon, long runs are important for many reasons. One of them is time. You need to learn what it feels like to be on your feet for three or four or five hours or however long it's going to take you to run 26 miles. It's psychological as much as physiological. You're developing your confidence each time you run long.

Time Zones

Racing away from home is fun, but crossing too many time zones can play havoc with your body clock. And jet lag can be compounded by the languor that follows a long plane ride. Some experts suggest arriving one day before the race for each time zone crossed, but this may be impracticable for busy people. Instead, avoid alcohol while in the air, but drink lots of other fluids. After you land, combine easy exercise (walking) with feet-up resting. Scheduling a massage for immediately after arrival is the best antidote to jet lag.

Too's

Running too far or too fast or too often can cause you to run slower in the marathon than if you run too little. Beware of too many *too's*.

Toughness

In the last mile of the marathon, you'll discover how tough you really are.

Tourist

Running marathons in different parts of the world can bring you to places you otherwise might never visit. But don't plan to race and go home without seeing the city you ran through. Be an intelligent tourist. Plan ahead. Study travel brochures. Arrive early enough that you can visit museums and participate in activities unique to the area. It will enhance the experience both for you and for those who accompany you.

Tracks

Almost all outdoor tracks are 400 meters around, about a quarter mile, four laps to the mile. Indoor tracks often are 200 meters (eight laps to the mile), but may vary greatly depending

(continued on page 185)

Taper Tips

1. Avoid panic: You can't make up for lost training. If you started late or lost time because of an injury, forget it. That one last hard workout may cause you to run slower in the marathon rather than faster.

2. Secure your gear: Have you replaced the high-mileage shoes you wore all through training? Do so well before race day to ensure a proper fit. Test your race uniform as well while there's still time to consider a replacement.

3. Beware taper madness: Cutting back on miles before the marathon is good for your legs, less so for your mind. Running can be addictive, so don't rush around doing silly things when you're supposed to be resting. Relax!

4. Eat carefully: Good nutrition is essential all during the training buildup, but it is particularly important the last three days before the marathon. Carbohydrates rule! But don't overeat, particularly while cruising the aisles at the Expo.

5. Get your rest: Getting a good night's sleep is most important on Friday, the night before the night before. On Saturday you may be too nervous to sleep well, plus you'll need to rise early. Catch your most Z's 48 hours out.

Do all this, and when the sun rises on marathon morning, you will almost certainly meet with success.

on the amount of space within the indoor facility. If you run in one of the outside lanes (often required at some tracks), you will run a somewhat longer distance. How much longer can be determined by examining the lane staggers near the starting line. If in doubt, ask the track coach in attendance.

Trails

One way to avoid injuries is to run on soft surfaces. The impact difference between concrete and grass is 16-fold. The perfect running surface is a golf course fairway, a gravel bike path or a smooth beach such as Ponte Vedra Beach in Florida where I train during the winter. But uneven surfaces, such as horse trails or loose sand, can cause more injuries than they cure. Make your move to soft surfaces gradual to give your muscles time to adapt to the extra twisting they may encounter. Eventually, running trails will make you a stronger runner.

Travel

Training while traveling is not easy, particularly if you're unfamiliar with running routes in cities you visit. Pick hotels in rural areas or near bodies of water (lakes or rivers), both for scenery and because fewer cross-streets make running easier.

Concierges in many hotels now provide maps. Use the fitness center to run on a treadmill or swim laps. Pack running gear in a separate bag. Run early to ensure completing your workout before business intrudes. Avoid difficult workouts, because travel imposes its own stress. Running through a new city often is the best way to see it.

Traffic Light

When stopped by a traffic light while running, don't compulsively jog in place feeling you need to stay in running mode. Relax. Rest. Use the time to stretch. Don't stop your watch to stay on pace, and don't cross through traffic at the risk of your life. *What's your hurry?* When the light turns green, you can go.

Trail Times

Never compare time and distance while training or racing on trails. Forget about how fast you might have run had you run the same distance on a smoother surface. If you want to run five miles, estimate the minutes it would take you to run that distance on the roads and run for about the same length of time. Soon you'll discover that you enjoy running off-road more than on the pavement. The variety will give both your mind and body a break.

Training

For many experienced runners, signing up for a marathon gives them an excuse to do what they want to do anyway: run lots of miles with a goal in sight. Thus, the training becomes as important as the race itself.

Treatment

Don't fool around if illness or an injury threatens while you're training for a marathon. See a podiatrist immediately for blisters or other foot problems. Schedule a massage or visit a physical therapist for muscle problems. You have too big a training investment, so don't delay.

The Trip

When you train for your first marathon, you will discover that life is about "The Trip" and not some final destination.

Tripping

The most efficient runners often skim the ground with their feet, lifting barely an inch or two off the ground. This is because lifting your feet too high wastes energy and slows you down. The down side of this efficiency is that even tiny obstacles encountered on the road or trail can trip you. Be very cautious while running over uneven ground so that you don't trip and injure yourself.

Truce

An uneasy truce exists between runners and those who exercise in other sports: walkers and cyclists and roller-bladers who use the same paths. If we all can learn the rules of our respective sports, as well as learning to respect each other—and those who do not exercise—we will be able to continue to enjoy the freedom of the road.

26 Miles

Running 26 miles at any pace is tough on the body. That's one reason I don't recommend going that far in practice. Long runs with a maximum length of 20 miles are more than sufficient to get most runners ready for a marathon. Inspiration during the race itself, plus the energy you store during a taper of several weeks, will permit you to jump the extra 6 miles to the finish line.

U

is for Uphill

189

The Ultimate

No matter what time you finish in your first marathon, you will look at that first 26-mile race as an ultimate experience. You may run faster in later marathons and achieve greater levels of success, but there is always something special about that first time.

Ultramarathons

Now that you've finished a few dozen marathons and reached a point at which performance improvements seem impossible, consider a further challenge. Try an ultra-marathon, a race beyond the 26-mile 385-yard distance. You'll find fewer people running in 50-K or 50-mile races, but they are a breed unto their own. Surprisingly, you don't need to train that much more. Restructuring your training to combine more long runs with more rest can help you succeed at ultra-marathon distances.

Underestimating Ability

Many beginners underestimate their abilities as athletes. Through proper training, you can discover new abilities you had not imagined were there.

Undertraining

While faint heart never won fair lady, you're usually better off arriving at a race undertrained rather than overtrained, particularly when it comes to the marathon.

Underwear

Most running shorts are designed with inner linings so you need not wear underwear beneath them. For women, however, an extra layer of fabric may protect their modesty or prevent infection. For men, extra support usually is not needed. Underwear beneath your shorts will only decrease your comfort and increase the risk of chafing. For women, sport bras offer not only more support but more comfort.

Underweight

Although the world's fastest marathoners are short and skinny and have low body-fat percentages, don't try to emulate them. Anorexia nervosa is a *very* serious problem, not only among teenage girls but also among others (even males) who compulsively diet to lose weight. If your body fat drops too low, not only will your performances nose-dive, you will permanently damage your health.

Unfairness

Some people are genetically more talented than others. It's called the Unfairness Syndrome. Genetics is the most important reason that some succeed and others fail. Training will get you only so far. Although qualifying for the Boston Marathon may be something you can only dream about, others train for only a few months and qualify in their first marathon. It *is* unfair! But relax, and enjoy running at your own level. Measure your success against yourself, not against others.

Unimportant

Personal Records. Age-group trophies. Finishing pictures on the wall. Plaudits. All such things are peripheral and unimportant. More important is how you feel each time you step out the door to run.

Uphill

When confronted by a hill, don't panic. Simply slow down. Cut your stride. Ignore well-meaning bystanders who tell you to "lean into the hill." Actually, proper form requires maintaining your body angle vs. the slope as close to 90 degrees as possible. Look toward the top of the hill rather than drop your head. That will prevent your form from deteriorating. Once atop the hill, you can resume your natural stride if the top is flat, or prepare for the descent.

Upper Body

Although running is a lower-body activity, don't overlook upper-body exercises in your training. Your arms provide at least a small part of your forward motion; once they fatigue, you won't run as fast. Strength training is important not merely for your success as a runner, but for your overall health. And don't overlook swimming as a great upper-body exercise that will strengthen you and relax you on off days.

Upper Respiratory Infections

Runners normally experience only half as many upper respiratory infections as the general population. This is because healthful living has its rewards. But runners lose some of this protection if we race frequently, and particularly if we run marathons. This is because extra training can depress our immune systems. Make mileage increases gradually to avoid making yourself a victim of upper respiratory illness.

Upside Down

Write the mile splits you want to hit upside down on your race number. That way you can check the time each mile and assure yourself that you are on pace.

Urination

Ducking into the bushes or waiting in line before a portable toilet during a marathon is a waste of time. The clock continues to tick while you pee. Learn how to manage fluids in and fluids out during your long training runs so that you won't have to stop to urinate. While experts say drink-drink-drink to avoid dehydration and overheating during a hot-weather marathon, it is possible to drink too much. Fluids drunk do you little good if they're running out of you.

V
is for Victory

Vacation

If on vacation, don't feel trapped by your training program. While visiting Yellowstone or Disney World with your family, don't obsess over running the same number of miles or doing the exact workouts you run at home. More important than what you do any day or week is consistency over months and years. If you're going to be on vacation or away on business trips, adjust your marathon schedule to fit your Real Life schedule, not the other way around.

Variation

Some variation in your training pace is normal. Don't expect every day's workout to be perfect. Weather, fatigue or the course you run can cause you to run slower or faster, so don't focus too much on time. To succeed in training, you need to be in the ballpark, not perched on the 50-yard line.

Victory

With the exception of one man—currently Khalid Khannouchi, the world-record holder—everyone else in the world is "slower." Few people lose in a marathon; we all just win with different times.

Videos

Use your video camera to improve your form, enlisting a friend to videotape you. One advantage of the current generation of video cameras is that you can employ stop-action to check your form at different stride points. The latest digital cameras allow you even to download these single-frame pictures into a computer and print them.

Viewing

I've watched marathons everywhere from the TV anchor desk (serving as commentator) to the press truck ahead of the runners (you see very little) to the sidelines (clever planning allows multiple viewing points) to the V.I.P. tent (enjoyable because you can eat and drink while watching the TV). The best view, however, is from inside the race: running the full 26 miles 385 yards.

Virginity

Make your first marathon easy, both training for it and racing in it. Pick a low-mileage plan. Set a time goal you can easily accomplish. Enjoy the sights and sounds and finish, knowing you could have run faster. There will be plenty of time to take marathon training more seriously later if you decide to run another.

Viruses

Serious illnesses involving viruses can haunt you for weeks. While you can continue to run if you have a bad cold, it's never wise to run if you have the flu, or any illness that causes an elevation in temperature. If a doctor prescribes antibiotics, that's another sign to take it easy. Get in bed, drink lots of fluids, and do *not* return to serious training until you're fully recovered. If you start running too soon, you can compromise your immune system and cause the illness to linger longer than if you did not run at all.

Visualization

Top athletes in many sports use visualization to mentally practice their disciplines. A bobsledder visualizes each turn in the track, running the course over and over in his mind. A basketball player sees the ball swooshing into the basket before he shoots a free throw. Runners can use this technique too, visualizing the last half-dozen miles of the marathon course and thinking of themselves crossing the finish line at their moment of victory.

Vitamins

The best way to get vitamins is as packaged in fruits and vegetables, mainly because of all the other beneficial substances contained in the package. These substances include minerals, fiber and antioxidants as well as neutraceuticals that show a relationship to the prevention of diseases, particularly cancer.

Volunteers

Without volunteers there would be no marathons; at least none of them could be conducted as successfully as they are now. Volunteers stuff bags, hand out T-shirts and stand along the course offering everything from water to cheers. At the LaSalle Bank Chicago Marathon, 7,000 volunteers support the 37,500 runners in the race. Some of these volunteers become inspired and run the marathon themselves the following year.

Vomiting

It doesn't happen often, but runners sometimes throw up after they cross the finish line. Often the problem is related to diet: what they ate or drank before or during the race. (Too much sugar can trigger nausea.) Vomiting also can be caused by nervousness. Bill Russell, the great Boston Celtics center, used to upchuck before every important game, but it didn't seem to slow down his play. As runners gain experience, vomiting should become less of a problem.

Vulnerability

Misjudge your training while preparing for a marathon and you will learn that the human body can withstand serious punishment, yet is so, so vulnerable.

W

is for
Warm-Up

Walking

There is no shame in walking during a marathon. There is disappointment or frustration only in not finishing. Walking early, before you are forced to, can help you continue a steady pace later in the race.

Walking Strategy

One strategy to use when walking in a marathon—either by design or out of despair—is that when you start to walk, look ahead and pick out the spot where you will begin running again. That ensures that you won't walk longer than necessary. If forced to walk again, even if after only a few running strides, pick another spot *immediately!*

Walk/Run

Walking during marathons and other distance events has proven popular among newcomers, who no longer feel obligated to run every step of the way. Rather than follow a rigid routine in which you walk every 10 minutes (or other precise time or mileage), plan your breaks around aid stations. Walking through aid stations allows you to drink more fully without spilling water on yourself or the ground. Whenever you walk, do so by the side of the road so that you don't block runners and make them dodge around you.

Warm-Up

It's a good idea to warm up before running, particularly before a hard workout or a race. Even jogging a half mile or so will warm your muscles. Follow that with some stretching, and you'll be ready to go.

Warm-Up (marathon)

While warming up (above) is an important pre-race and pre-workout strategy, achieving that end may be impossible in a big city marathon with 10,000 or more runners crowding the starting grid. If so, do the best you can. Jogging a short distance an hour before the marathon can, if nothing else, loosen your bowels and help avoid a mid-race potty break. Lack of warm-up is all the more reason to run slowly during the first few miles of a marathon.

Waste

Training for a marathon can teach you how much time you waste doing little of consequence. An hour spent watching

TV becomes a 7-mile run. Time wasted daydreaming becomes time spent in the morning sun. It's all about setting priorities for the time you have available in your life.

Watches

Having a watch that allows you to record each mile split in a workout or in the marathon race itself is a good motivational tool. You can use it to see if you're on schedule. Afterward, you can check the watch to analyze how the workout or race went. But don't be a slave to your watch and the splits it provides. In bad weather or on tough courses, following a set time plan can get you in trouble by making you run too fast.

Weather

When planning to run a marathon, check the weather reports—then forget them. It can turn suddenly cold in summer or warm in winter, often without warning. Go to the race prepared for almost every weather condition. This may mean packing more clothes than normal. Even if it's cold when you leave your house to drive to the starting line, it may be hot when you finish. If you go to the race expecting to be surprised by a change in the weather, you will never be surprised.

Weekends

Most runners have more time to train on weekends. It's easier to do the long runs and recover from them if you don't have to jump in a car or board a bus to be at work before 9:00. Most training schedules are planned to reflect that reality. But if a different day works best for you, change the schedule. The overall pattern of how you train over a long period of time is more important than what you do for any one workout and when you do it.

Whether

Whether it's hot or cold, whether it's raining or snowing, whether the weather is good or bad—weather can affect your day's training plan. Maintain consistent training over a long period of time, and you won't need to worry what the weatherman serves you.

Why

Mountain climber Robert Mallory (when asked why he wanted to climb Mount Everest) responded: "Because it is there." That response seems to satisfy mountain climbers, but maybe not always marathoners. For many soon-to-be runners, participating in a marathon seems a very ambitious, distant and even glorious goal, yet one that is attainable. Different runners have different reasons for wanting to run 26 miles 385 yards, and those reasons often change from marathon to marathon.

Will

You can't run a good marathon without preparing for it carefully. Near the end of the marathon—if you haven't trained properly—there is a lack of will to run fast, or maybe even to finish.

Wind

When training, check the wind before choosing the direction you run. It's best to start running *into* a stiff wind so that you have it at your back at the end of the workout, when you will be more fatigued. This is particularly important during winter, since you may be finishing soaked with sweat.

Withdrawal

When runners hit the peak of their training and start to taper for their race—particularly if they do a long taper of several weeks before a marathon—they often begin to feel sluggish and antsy. These are typical withdrawal symptoms and are as much psychological as physical. You miss your longer runs and maybe the time spent with training companions. But any anxiety you may feel is a small price to pay for race-day achievement.

X-Y-Z

is for X-Rays, Youth and The Zone

Generation X

As recently as 1950, only a few hundred runners participated in the Boston Marathon, and there was only a handful of other considerably smaller marathons elsewhere in the U.S. Women never ran marathons in that era and, in fact, were prohibited! The second half of the century, however, saw a surge in marathon interest, particularly among members of Generation X. As we move into the new millennium, there are hundreds of marathons; fields of 25,000 or more are not uncommon. Not only are more people in their 20s running marathons, but many of them are female.

X-Rays

X-rays are not always satisfactory for diagnosing running injuries, which often occur to soft tissue. Even with a stress fracture, it often takes several weeks after the break for calcification of the bone to signal that a fracture took place. An experienced sports-medicine professional often can learn more by asking you questions about your injuries than by using high-priced diagnostic machines.

Yasso Repeats

This form of speed training was the brainchild of Bart Yasso, a promotion director for *Runner's World* magazine. Yasso theorized that you could run 10 × 800 (with a brief rest between each repeat) with the same numbers as your marathon time. In other words, a 3:00 marathoner (three hours) should do 800s in 3:00 (three minutes). A 3:30 marathoner, 3:30 800s, and so forth. It's a training gimmick, yes, but somehow it works.

Youth

The best way to retain your youth is to exercise, and the best way to exercise is to run. You'll look better. You'll feel better. And when you tell people your age, they'll be amazed at how youthful you seem.

Z's

Getting a good night's sleep is most important on Friday, the night before the night before a Sunday marathon. Saturday you may be too nervous to sleep well, and you'll need to rise early. Catch your most Z's 48 hours out.

Zigzag

Failing to train for long periods of time is not a good idea unless you're recuperating after an injury or recovering (mentally as well as physically) from a marathon. Rest days are necessary, but research suggests that, over time, every day of missed training requires two days of running to regain the lost fitness. That suggests it will take you four weeks to regain what you give away in two weeks. Training at a steady level allows you to accomplish more compared to zigzagging back and forth between hard training and nothing.

The Zone

Various fad diets that promote high-protein or low-carbohydrate regimens are *disastrous* for endurance athletes. The so-called "Zone" or 40/30/30 diets (40 percent carbohydrate, 30 percent fat, 30 percent protein) don't provide enough carbs to replace the glycogen you burn during training. A healthier mix is 55/30/15. Research promoting these fad diets is flawed. If you want to lose weight, either eat less or exercise more, or do both. It's difficult, if not impossible, to train adequately for a marathon while on a low-carbohydrate diet. You'll be in a Zone, but in the wrong zone for finishing the race comfortably.

Marathon Resources

Finding what you need to know about this 26-mile sport

I often appear at pre-race events, most regularly at the Expo before The LaSalle Bank Chicago Marathon. Because so many runners training for that marathon use my schedules, crowds in front of my booth cram the aisles. I chat with runners, pose for photos and autograph copies of my books.

Runners frequently ask for recommendations: Which book to buy? For most at marathons, my knee-jerk response is: *Marathon: The Ultimate Training Guide.* That's my best-seller. Originally published in 1993, I revised and updated it a half-dozen years later to reflect the many changes in our sport at the start of a new century: everything from sport gels to chip timing to 30,000-plus fields. I hope I'm not being too self-centered when I say that every marathon runner should own a copy of *Marathon: The Ulti-*

mate Training Guide. Second choice for those who want to improve their marathon times while competing at shorter distances would be my *Run Fast*.

But there are many other resources that you should consider if your goal is success and enjoyment running 26 miles 385 yards. Visit my Web site: www.halhigdon.com for training programs and articles on everything from strength to stretching to nutrition. Most popular among those who surf into the site is my 18-week marathon-training program with five separate levels, one for novices and two each for intermediate and advanced runners. If you want to ask me a question, you can do so on *Virtual Training*, accessible free from www.halhigdon.com and www.chicagomarathon.com. This is the domain of my "V-Team," and I'll often answer as many as 20 or 30 questions a day. Many of the tips offered in this book evolved from those answers. Here are some sources for marathon runners, prepared with the help of my V-Team:

Books

Someone who has been in the running trenches with me for more than four decades (we first met in 1960) is Joe Henderson, who writes a monthly column for *Runner's World*. I asked Joe which of his many books he would recommend, and he suggested *Marathon Training*. Another of Joe's books that I frequently pull off the shelf for help answering questions about injuries is one he co-authored with podiatrist Joe Ellis, D.P.M.: *Running Injury Free*. Most recently, Joe co- authored *The Runner's Encyclopedia* with Rich Benyo, editor of *Marathon & Beyond*.

Another *Runner's World* columnist who has trained thousands of marathon runners is Jeff Galloway. Check out his *Marathon!* Two books by Bob Glover, *The Runner's Handbook* and *The Competitive Runner's Handbook,* were written several decades ago but continue to sell in revised editions. Gordon Bakoulis-Bloch's *How to Train for and Run Your Best Marathon* includes a special section for women. Dave Kuehls' *4 Months to a 4-Hour Marathon* promises success.

Consider also *Lore of Running* by Tim Noakes, M.D., a sports-medicine specialist from The University of Cape Town Medical School in South Africa. At 804 pages, Timmy's book contains an amazing amount of scientific information while introducing you to legendary runners such as Arthur Newton, called by world-record holder Ron Clarke "the greatest runner ever seen."

Nutrition is essential to marathon success. Liz Applegate and Nancy Clark have written compelling books on this subject. Check out Liz's *Eat Smart, Play Hard* for information on race-day strategies, recovery eating and what to eat depending upon the time you train during the day. There's also a chapter on running a marathon. *Nancy Clark's Sports Nutrition Guidebook* will provide further help in fueling you for peak performance.

Dr. George Sheehan inspired an entire generation of runners who came of age in the late 1970s. Among his many books, *This Running Life* may be the best, with *Running and Being: The Total Experience* a close second. I wrote the postscript for Frank Murphy's obscure but moving *A Cold, Clear Day*, about Buddy Edelen, the American who in 1963 set the world marathon record.

Magazines

Let's begin with *Runner's World*. With a U.S. circulation over half a million and separate editions in a half-dozen foreign countries, *Runner's World* (33 East Minor Street, Emmaus, PA 18098; 800–666–2828; www.runnersworld.com) dominates the market, with *Running Times* (213 Danbury Road, Wilton, CT 06897; 203–761–1113; www.runningtimes.com) a distant second. Both magazines devote a lot of their pages to training advice for the marathon and shorter events. More tightly focused on long-distance running is the bi-monthly *Marathon and Beyond* (206 N. Randolph, Suite 502, Champaign, IL 61820; 877–972–4230; www.marathonandbeyond.com). At the other end of the sport is *Track & Field News* (2570 El Camino Real, Suite 606, Mountain View, CA 94040; 650–948–8188; www.trackandfieldnews.com), with marathoning only a small part of its editorial package. The same is true of *National Masters News* (PO Box 50098, Eugene, OR 97401; 541–343–7716; www.nationalmastersnews.com), aimed at competitive athletes over the age of 40. Many running clubs (see below) publish their own newsletters, and various regional magazines serve specific areas. Plug into the club network in your area, and you can find them.

Organizations

The Road Runners Club of America (1150 S. Washington Street, Alexandria, VA 22314; 703–836–0558) publishes a quarterly magazine titled *footnotes*, but that organization is perhaps most vital as a source for leads to its more than 700 running clubs and 200,000 individual members. If you want to make contact with runners who share your same training paths, there probably is an RRCA club near you. To find it, log onto www.rrca.com and go to the section that lists clubs by geographical location. I go this route often when I am traveling in unfamiliar areas and need to find training partners, running routes or races.

Although it's no longer necessary to belong to USA Track and Field to enter the Boston Marathon or other major marathons, a few national and international races require membership in USATF (1 RCA Dome, Suite 140, Indianapolis, IN 46225; 317–261–0500; www.usatf.com). The USATF Web site provides links to many other running-related sites.

Web sites

An enormous amount of information of interest to marathoners is available on the World Wide Web. I am a regular visitor to *Runner's World Daily News* (www.runnersworld.com) for race results and commentary on our sport, but most valuable to marathoners is a calendar listing every U.S. marathon and many major international races. Look also for the "Tools" section that allows you to enter your 5-K time, for example, and project how fast you should be able to run a marathon. The training programs I authored for *Runner's World*'s online edition are somewhat less complete than those you will find on my own Web site (www.halhigdon.com), but there are numerous other articles on training worth viewing. Want to know how to run Yasso 800s? The information is there.

Another Web cornucopia that includes schedules of races and training information is *Marathon Guide* (www.marathon guide.com). For fans of Dr. Sheehan, his Web site (www. georgesheehan.com) contains dozens of George's essays. In-grid Kristiansen, the Norwegian runner whose world record of 2:21:05 lasted more than a decade, has a Web site (www. ingridkristiansen.com) that promotes holistic fitness and marathon running. Many competitive runners have their own Web sites, including marathon world-record holder Khalid Khannouchi (www.khannouchi.com).

For information on international running, go to *Run The Planet* (www.runtheplanet.org), which bills itself as "the largest worldwide running community on the Internet." That seems a stretch, but it's probably true. The site boasts 2,287 descriptions of where to run and walk in 1,793 cities around the world.

When you're looking for shoes, nothing beats a specialty running store, such as Fleet Feet in Chicago, where Dave and

Lisa Zimmer will provide hands-on service. But if you want to shop online, try Road Runner Sports (www.roadrunnersports.com). Most of the major running-shoe companies have Web sites that sometimes feature training advice, for example www.newbalance.com. Many running Web sites provide links to other running Web sites. Here's a good place to start: www.hillrunner.com. For an amazing amount of information related to the competitive aspects of running, see www.letsrun.com.

Most marathons also provide Web sites that offer not only detailed information about their event but also allow you to enter online. You can find these sites easily by doing a search featuring the race name, or linking from one of the calendars mentioned above. Many major marathons also have training programs, such as the CARA (Chicago Area Running Association) Marathon Training Class in which I participate to prepare runners for The LaSalle Bank Chicago Marathon. We work with 2,000 runners each summer in five clinic locations and nine workout locations. We feel we're the best, but we're not unique. Several charities have training programs. The largest is the Leukemia & Lymphoma Society's Team in Training (TNT). In 2000, 35,000 TNT runners raised $82.4 million for the organization. You see their purple singlets in marathons everywhere. Other privately run training programs are The Kenyan Way (4400 Memorial Drive, Suite 3010, Houston, TX 77007; 713–864–8872; www.kenyanway.com); USAFIT (5100 Westheimer, Suite 200, Houston, TX 77056; www.usafit.com); and the programs of Jeff Galloway (Galloway Productions, 4651 Roswell Road, I-802, Atlanta, GA 30342; www.jeffgalloway.com).

Never before has it been easier to become a marathoner. You still need to do the training and run the race—and that's not necessarily easy—but information on how to do it is accessible for all those who look.

Bibliography

APPLEGATE, LIZ, Ph.D. *Eat Smart, Play Hard*. Emmaus, Pennsylvania: Rodale Press, 2001.

BAKOULIS-BLOCH, GORDON. *How to Train for and Run Your Best Marathon*. New York: Simon & Schuster, 1993.

BENYO, RICH, WITH JOE HENDERSON. *The Runner's Encyclopedia*. Champaign, Illinois: Human Kinetics, 2001.

CLARK, NANCY, M.S., R.D. *Nancy Clark's Sports Nutrition Guidebook*, Champaign, Illinois: Hunan Kinetics, 1997.

ELLIS, JOE, D.P.M., WITH JOE HENDERSON. *Running Injury Free*. Emmaus, Pennsylvania: Rodale Press, 1994.

GALLOWAY, JEFF. *Marathon!* Atlanta, Georgia: Phidippides Press, 2000.

GLOVER, BOB, WITH JACK SHEPHERD AND SHELLY GLOVER. *The Runner's Handbook*. New York: Penguin Books, 1977, 1996.

GLOVER, BOB, WITH JACK SHEPHERD. *The Competitive Runner's Handbook.* New York: Penguin Books, 1983, 1999.

HENDERSON, JOE. *Marathon Training.* Champaign, Illinois: Human Kinetics, 1997.

KUEHLS, DAVE. *4 Months to a 4-Hour Marathon.* New York: Perigree, 1998.

MURPHY, FRANK. *A Cold, Clear Day.* Kansas City, Missouri: Wind Sprint Press, 1992.

NOAKES, TIM, M.D. *Lore of Running.* Champaign, Illinois, Leisure Press, 1991.

SHEEHAN, GEORGE A., M.D. *Running and Being: The Total Experience.* Red Bank, New Jersey: Second Wind II, LLC, 1998.

SHEEHAN, GEORGE A., M.D. *This Running Life.* New York: Simon and Schuster, 1980.

Index